DATE DUE

What Our Stories Teach Us

A Guide to Critical Reflection for College Faculty

Linda K. Shadiow

JOSSEY-BASS
A Wiley Imprint
www.josseybass.com

Published by Jossey-Bass

A Wiley Imprint

One Montgomery Street, Suite 1200, San Francisco, CA 94104-4594—www.josseybass.com

Jossey-Bass books and products are available through most bookstores. To contact Jossey-Bass directly call our Customer Care Department within the U.S. at 800-956-7739, outside the U.S. at 317-572-3986, or fax 317-572-4002.

Wiley publishes in a variety of print and electronic formats and by print-on-demand. Some material included with standard print versions of this book may not be included in e-books or in print-on-demand. If this book refers to media such as a CD or DVD that is not included in the version you purchased, you may download this material at http://booksupport.wiley.com. For more information about Wiley products, visit www.wiley.com.

Library of Congress Cataloging-in-Publication Data

Shadiow, Linda K., 1947–
    What our stories teach us : a guide to critical reflection for college faculty /
Linda K. Shadiow.
        pages cm – (The Jossey-Bass higher and adult education series)
    Includes bibliographical references and index.
    ISBN 978-1-118-10329-6 (cloth), 978-1-118-41620-4 (ebk.),
    978-1-118-41877-2 (ebk.), 978-1-118-55402-9 (ebk.)
    1. College Teaching.
    LB2331 .S4725 2013

                                                            2012048916

Printed in the United States of America

FIRST EDITION

HB Printing 10 9 8 7 6 5 4 3 2 1

The Jossey-Bass
Higher and Adult Education Series

Contents

Preface   vii

Acknowledgments   xv

About the Author   xix

1. Storied Contexts   3
2. Living Stories   25
3. Storied Accounts   45
4. Seeking Patterns   65
5. Exploring Patterns   85
6. Locating Assumptions   103
7. Exploring Paradigmatic Assumptions   125
8. Storied Teaching   149

References   171

Index   179

Preface

A few years ago Sharon, my former graduate school office mate, and I were walking in the high country desert talking about our careers as college teachers. When rare opportunities like this arise, we often exchange stories about the avenues we are trying to open up for strengthening student learning. At the same time that we wound our way around a barely visible path, we also found ourselves on a path moving from current to more distant and less-visible stories. The contemporary incidents we began with kept reminding us of earlier stories from our teaching.

Not long after we shared offices in graduate school, I published a brief essay, "My Students as My Teachers" (1985). The essay consisted of a series of brief vignettes about how the students in classes I had as a teaching assistant contributed to my emerging knowledge of college teaching. In the decades since then I have become increasingly curious about why certain stories stay with me and why I find occasions to either write about them, tell them to others, or reflect on them when some current spark ignites a memory. I wonder what stories have accompanied you along the way, what stories reappear as you recall or possibly retell them? I wonder, what is it about these incidents that keeps them always within our reach?

One of these stories for me is a simple one about a conference over a grade on a student paper. Kirby, or so I called him in that

1985 essay, was a student in the first class I taught as a graduate teaching assistant.

The students in the freshman composition course came in one morning and retrieved their graded papers from a stack on the front desk. Kirby approached me—graded paper in hand—and said he wanted to come to my office after class to discuss his grade. At the end of the class period after the other students had filed out, he followed me to my office as I was trying silently to recall the grade on his paper. There was no conversation in the hallway, and the elevator ride was awkwardly silent. Only his clenched jaw and determined stance spoke. He was, I surmised, rehearsing what he would say to me.

Since this early experience I have read the literature on the benefits of reflecting on teaching. I have done so while seeking to understand how the choices I make in instances such as this one can create either some positive results or negative consequences for learners as well as for me. My reflection has taken the form of replaying classroom incidents in my head while rewriting the scripts, talking with colleagues, and submitting a few personal essays like "My Students as My Teachers" (1985) to professional journals. But it was during an afternoon conversation with a friend twenty some years after I had met Kirby that led to my seeing stories as something other than sentimental anecdotes with thinly veiled lessons.

Kirby's story stood out for me initially because of the unexpected reason for his request to talk.

Once Kirby and I entered my office he put his paper on my desk and I saw a red-circled "A." "I have never been an 'A' student," he declared. He explained that in order to get B's and C's on his essays he had relied on his wife's help. Because he had written this paper without her assistance, he concluded the grade was a mistake. I had two immediate reactions—astonishment and relief. Without expressing either of these to him, I carefully went through the paper pointing out its strengths. He stared at me, obviously uncertain about how to respond. Eventually he stood up, thanked me for taking the time, and left the office still shaking his head.

As I saw it then, being Kirby's teacher meant the merits of my judgment should not be open to challenge for any reason. Kirby's role was to learn from my judgments, not to question them. I was not looking for dialogue of any kind. Classrooms, I believed, were intended as places for monologue where any hint at dialogue contained the threat of a challenge. As a new college teacher, I was seeking to avoid any such threat to my relatively slim margin of confidence. I have come to revisit this story in succeeding years, and each time I do I gain insights not possible at the time the incident happened. My fear as we walked back to my office that day, I think, was that classroom control could slip from my grasp. As you revisit stories from your own educational biographies throughout this book, there will be many opportunities to review stories for what new considerations analysis can reveal. One of the goals in this book is to provide "company along the way" (Welch, 1999, p. xvi) as you recall, retell, and then scrutinize your stories.

By revisiting this simple story over the years and by including it along with other stories as a part of a reflective process, I have come to see that it holds multiple surprises. In addition to the surprise reason Kirby had for asking to speak with me about his grade, after years of teaching I can acknowledge that my response focused on me rather than on him. At the moment I realized he was contesting an "A," I was relieved not to have to defend myself in the same way I would have if his grade had been lower than he expected. I emerged from the office conference with my sense of control and authority firmly in place. As I continue to include this story with others in an ongoing process of reflection today, it contains much to help me learn about the ongoing presence of themes of control and authority in my work.

During our autumn walk my colleague and I talked about stories and insights such as this one. She urged me to merge my interest in stories with my interest in reflection. Here, she suggested, was a chance to explore the question that had been an inherent part of our conversations over the years since graduate school, and this has now become a central question of this book: "How can our growth as college teachers be aided by critical reflection on stories in our educational biographies?"

My stories like "Kirby's Paper" are woven throughout the following chapters in order to share with you the process that this book invites you to undertake. And there is a conclusion to Kirby's story. When I wrote the vignette, I relayed one last portion of the incident. At that time it had a single meaning, and now I can see another. Here is how Kirby's story ended for that semester and what I concluded at the time.

At the conclusion of the course Kirby proudly showed me a letter-to-the-editor he wrote for a class assignment that was published in a local magazine—the same magazine where his wife, a freelance writer, had a feature story published. At the end of my 1985 essay that included this incident, I commented that Kirby "taught me labels aren't forever" (p. 332).

I have come to see that there is an underlying story here that I initially overlooked. How I prescribed teacher and student roles actually framed how I experienced and now how I retell "Kirby's Paper." This teaches me that my expectations for student-teacher interactions rested on my view of those individual roles, but those roles "aren't forever." The project of this book is to begin with a recollection of just such stories.

The impetus for the book came from my ongoing commitment to being a better college teacher, a commitment I share with friends, colleagues, and many readers. We seek ways to understand college teaching. Many calls for reflection begin by directing us to take a careful look at classroom techniques we choose and actions we take in response to classroom events. The literature suggests that we do this through processes like keeping journals, thinking deeply about our practices, and considering feedback from students and colleagues. Although this book does not include a comprehensive review of this literature, it does draw on the classic and contemporary resources in building a process that speaks to the needs and benefits that such literature on reflection identifies. Moving from a desire to reflect critically on our teaching to actually doing so is something we will undertake together. Through understanding our own educational biographies we have the potential to illuminate our current work and its future directions. This book explores what I've discovered and what I believe is there for all teachers to uncover in their stories.

Chapter Overview

The ways that stories are built into the daily aspects of college teaching frame the recognition of our lives as story-builders. Amid the daily press of routines we are unacknowledged authors of stories in our classrooms and research, during office conferences, and in our hallway conversations. The stories embedded within our life-long educational experiences are a part of how we author our daily stories, but subconsciously so. The context for this book's three-stage process of reflection on what our stories teach us is provided in Chapter One with an exploration of the ways in which story-building and story-telling are an inherent element in college teaching. Such contexts raise questions about what stories we *bring* to this work.

Using the contexts explored in Chapter One as a backdrop, Chapters Two and Three prompt the recapturing of past stories, those that come easily to mind like "Kirby's Paper" and those that we remember when we take the focused time to do so. Stage One in the reflective process in these two chapters includes collecting a repertoire of stories that are a part of how we tell ourselves and others about our teacher-selves. Within that repertoire are key anecdotes—critical incidents—with an emotional pull that sets them apart from other stories. While the stories play a role in reflection, the critical incidents identified in Chapter Three become the primary focus of attention for subsequent stages.

Measured by the reflective coding process I outline in this book, the "Kirby's Paper" story, while being memorable for me, does not reach a threshold of being a *critical incident*. It does, however, resonate with some of the underlying themes and assumptions that are revealed through an analysis of my critical incidents. Throughout the book I draw on critical incidents from my own repertoire of stories like "First Day," "Students Applaud Students," and "Shoulder-Shrugger" to bring the process of critical reflection into focus so others can learn from an analysis of their own.

Given a flourish of details that emerge around critical incidents in Stage One, the second stage invites the reader to consider the stories in unexpected ways. There is an iridescent quality to the critical incidents, as insights are gained in Chapters Four and Five. Insights garnered from one story refract off of the others as our angle of view shifts. The shifts come with looking at the presence of the students, teachers, and content in the critical incidents, and this enables a move from first seeing the stories as anecdotes to then acknowledging them as ancestors whom we have forgotten as a part of our professional family tree.

Chapters Six and Seven—Stage Three—move to a process of inviting the search for three levels of assumptions influencing our work. Stage Three engages the questions about where a pursuit of our stories' roots can lead and what is found there. The concluding chapter circles back to the repertoire of stories identified earlier in the book and traces the connections from the stories we bring to the stories we build.

The process, while laid out in a linear fashion, involves more choreography than a dance-step diagram drawn out on a floor. By providing a guided invitation to reflect on stories undergirding our practices, this book accompanies readers on pathways that are defined by readers themselves. The three-stage process is an invitation to take a guided opportunity to consider personal touchstones that suggest ways to proceed in our teaching practices. It is not likely for us to have looked at a collection of our stories to see where their details offer dissonance or resonance, nor to have considered linking threads in a repertoire of our stories to see how we have developed as college teachers. Doing this seeks to build on the heart of curiosity, wonder, and commitment which we bring to our profession.

A Note to Readers

This book is recursive, with each chapter building on the previous ones and later chapters returning to earlier ones to glean additional insights. Given that, the process of moving to deeper understanding is built chapter by chapter and will be most productive when worked through in that way. The series of prompts point to stages, but the time, space, and approach necessary to proceed are so personal that they need to be individualized by each reader. The prompts, therefore, are issued as invitations. I invite you to guide yourself through the process, responding to a series of prompts in ways you find personally meaningful. You may choose to jot notes down at each step in order to reconsider them throughout the process, or you may elect to work through charts or diagrams or sketches (narrative or artistic). The work will ask you to trust yourself in finding the mix of approaches you use. Similarly, and at various times, you may find working in solitude will serve your process, and at other times you may be drawn to talking with others, telling stories you are remembering or exploring insights you are finding.

At each stage, woven into the process are examples from a variety of disciplines. Teachers of geology, sociology, business, education, and English, for example, have written essays in professional journals, which I use as illustrations of different junctures in the reflective process set out in the book. No matter what the discipline, the work of college teaching draws on a commitment to student learning, but one that is fed by a wellspring of stories.

The intended readers of this book are college teachers from all disciplines. Readers for whom teaching is a source of commitment, wonder, and curiosity will find avenues for exploring those qualities. The book may be a source for use by individual faculty members pursuing a deepening understanding of their teaching, but it may be used with one or more colleagues, or even by a group in a professional development setting. It can be used in a mix—sometimes in solitude and sometimes in shared settings. Graduate students in a class where they are reflecting on the origins of their teaching philosophies and commitments to the college teaching profession may also be guided in that search.

There are, I am sure, uses beyond these few that are mentioned because the book involves a personal dialogue with oneself—the choices about how and when to engage others in that dialogue are many. Like on the afternoon walks where my colleague and I continually share stories and pose questions about their presence and persistence, there is the need for a path to follow, even a faint one. This book was written to provide such an opportunity, but readers of this book are its coauthors. What can you learn from your own stories, as I did from "Kirby's Paper," when you look more closely at them? How do they grow in meaning with each telling? I invite you to begin.

Acknowledgments

Y *oin* (yoh-EEN) is a Japanese word whose literal meaning is "re-verberations that continue for a long time after a well-cast bell is struck" (Rheingold, 1988, p. 142). I found it in a collection of words and phrases for which there are no direct English transla-tions (*They Have a Word for It*). I turned to this book because I was inarticulate in the face of trying to express my gratitude to those who have helped this book come to fruition. What I came up with ("there are no words to express my gratitude") fails to capture the depth of impact and influence a wonderful collection of friends and colleagues have had on this work. In Rheingold's book, he attempts to translate the applied meaning of the word as it might be ex-pressed in English: "Experiential reverberations that continue to move you long after the stimulus has ceased" (p. 142). It is in this sense that *yoin* begins to capture the extent of the impact of those involved in bringing this book to light. It is a privilege to acknowl-edge some of them here.

Countless numbers of students and teachers are at the marrow of this work. They have made innumerable contributions to my teaching, my thinking about teaching, and my writing about col-lective explorations of the students and teachers in my educational autobiography. I thank them for their patience and tolerance as I continue to grow in my work because of them.

Northern Arizona University was supportive in multiple ways. A sabbatical leave enabled me to give focused attention to this project, and the responsiveness of Cline Library to my requests for materials made it possible to do this work from a distance. During my sabbatical I was fortunate enough to have had brief residencies at Montana State University through the support of Carl Fox, and at Bemidji State University, with thanks to Joe Czapiewski for assisting with my last-minute request. NAU colleagues Susanna Maxwell, Cathy Small, Susan Longerbeam, Ro Haddon, and Gretchen McAllister have lent pivotal support for these ideas as they have evolved over a decade. For more years than most people know, Dan Kain and I have been colleagues, and his engagement in classrooms has enriched my own. Sharon Fagan's and my enduring friendship began when Professor Robert Shafer insightfully assigned us to share an office in graduate school at Arizona State. Since then she has been a formative influence on my trying to put into words the work we started doing when we taught English there. As the copy editor for early drafts, Eve Paulden had a sharp eye and approached the work with a combination of skill and care. When David Brightman of Jossey-Bass spoke to me at the earliest stage of the book, his enthusiasm and confidence fed my own. Maryellen Weimer is far more than a consulting editor. She was an early advocate who skillfully mentored me in the process of writing this book and has shepherded the development of its ideas; her guidance is present on every page, and our friendship extends beyond them. I am grateful to those I have mentioned here and countless others because in large and small ways they have made *yoin* a palpable reality in my life and work.

Even the concept of *yoin* cannot capture the profound influence my husband Bob Shadiow's partnership has had on my life. When I decided to move ahead in putting my ideas into a book his response was, "It's about time." As he has done throughout my career, he listened to my reading of each chapter multiple times with an ear toward making the ideas come alive with clarity and passion.

He unquestioningly supported my need for early morning solitude (and more bookshelves), and he provided balance with his insistence that we take walks even as I used those walks to untangle some of the ideas I was working on. His insight and support are present throughout the book. In fact, he is the author of the last line. And its sentiment is dedicated to him.

About the Author

Linda Shadiow came to her work as the director of faculty development at Northern Arizona University through a variety of avenues. She began her teaching career in a rural Minnesota community, moved to high school English teaching in Montana, and then worked as the English/language arts coordinator in the Montana Department of Public Instruction. She pursued graduate study in English and education at Montana State University and received her PhD from Arizona State University in 1982. She then returned to Montana as an English professor and during that time spent a year collaborating with a physics professor on a television series that focused on translating academic research for a general audience.

She accepted a position as associate executive director of the Center for Excellence in Education at Northern Arizona University (NAU) in 1985, where she is now a professor of educational foundations and director of the university's faculty development program. She has published widely and spoken extensively throughout her career with increasing attention to the stories that shape curriculum and instruction. She has been honored as NAU's faculty scholar of the year, administrator of the year, one of the Centennial Class of 100 representing key faculty who contributed to the university's first century, commencement speaker, and President's Award recipient, and has been named as one of the Outstanding Alumni of her undergraduate alma mater, Bemidji State University. Her university office recently relocated to the library at NAU, and as a consequence she is the proud holder of a key to the library.

What Our Stories Teach Us

Storied Contexts

"All there is to thinking," he said, "is seeing something noticeable which makes you see something you weren't noticing which makes you see something that isn't even visible."

(Maclean, 1976, p. 92)

On a plane to Phoenix, the woman sitting next to me turned and initiated introductions. Then she asked the usual follow-up question: "What do you do?" I responded, "I am a university professor." Instead of the critique of contemporary education I have come to expect in such situations, she asked, "When was it that you decided to become a teacher?" There were a few perfunctory responses I could have made, but instead, I found myself telling her a familiar story (Shadiow, 2009):

Winter Saturday Classroom

I was about ten years old when I remember trying out and liking the role of "teacher." During the bitter cold winter afternoons on the Iron Range in Northern Minnesota my parents expected me to keep my four younger siblings from getting underfoot in our small house. On many of those Saturdays, I willingly corralled my brother and sisters into my brother's bedroom, which doubled as our playroom, and directed them to sit behind the metal TV trays I had set up in rows of two so we could "play school." I relished leading an afternoon of lessons: there were well-worn Golden Books to guide their reading assignments, hand-printed spelling and vocabulary lists I had prepared to address their literacy deficiencies, and even math and science worksheets from my own elementary school class work to round out the curriculum. Just as I had suspected—being the teacher was more fun than being the student. I got to pick out who was recognized to speak, I could give permission (or not) for one of them to go to the bathroom, I could reward behavior with gold stars, and on occasion discipline inattention by whacking them over their head with damp mittens. I was in charge, and I liked it.

My airplane seatmate and I shared a laugh and moved to talking about her job. Then we each lowered our tray tables, an ironic echo of the TV trays in those winter Saturday classrooms, and we proceeded to focus on the very work we had just spoken about.

There are three stories here: the story of the plane conversation, the story of my first attempts at teaching, and, less visible, the story of the "teaching school" itself—why was this the reminiscence I chose to tell? I have asked my siblings if they remembered my initial attempts at teaching—they do. I have asked them if they ever told their own story about those experiences—they have not. And now that I am a professor, what is it about this "Winter Saturday Classroom" story that not only has me remembering the details, but has me regularly retelling them? To paraphrase Maclean's words introducing this chapter, When I see something I am not noticing, I am led to see something that isn't even visible. Our stories have lives beyond the moments of their retelling.

I have learned that the process of recalling, retelling, scrutinizing, and analyzing these stories sheds new light on my teaching. This process invites me into a level of reflection resembling the nested Russian folk dolls where opening one reveals another and opening that one reveals yet another. The stories included here are among those that have enabled me to go "assumption hunting" (Brookfield, 1995), to undertake the task of reflecting on my actions in teaching (Schön, 1983), and to go "inward bound" in order to understand the "outward bound" (Palmer, 2007). My stories are intended to illustrate directions such an uncovering can take and to guide your engagement in a similar process. In doing this I refer to stories like "Winter Saturday Classroom" multiple times to show how my understanding of its impact changes. The challenge of paying attention to the autobiographical roots of educational practices is only rarely taken up in university settings (Greene, 1973), no more so now than when Greene made that observation forty years ago. We are most likely to reflect on individual events than we are on the patterns shared by such events.

Most of us find ourselves testing out and then sharing stories about the use of successful classroom strategies or assignments with another faculty member. When faculty colleagues do the same, we may reflect on the extent to which the strategies they describe are applicable to our own work. We are unlikely, however, to think about the shifting patterns in our teaching that the addition of new teaching techniques or the elimination of old ones precipitates. Doing so, moving more deeply into the nesting of stories, can precipitate an awareness of how our perspectives have come to be shaped.

Shifting Perspectives

There are clichés that characterize overarching shifts in teaching: moving from "sage on the stage" to "guide on the side" is a common example. Recently, a business professor described this transition by characterizing himself initially as an "imposter with the roster," hiding behind an authoritarian persona but trying to move beyond being that "sage on the stage" (Starcher, 2010, p. 1). In this sense, Professor Starcher builds a new classroom story, and he tells that story to readers of the *Teaching Professor* (and likely to colleagues, family members, or maybe even strangers on planes).

Like Professor Starcher, we experience our careers as a process. Through this process we build a collection of stories that are indelible enough for us to tell others. We are not likely to consider, however, the role that these stories can play both in framing our teaching and in providing us with insights into the *origins* of our past, current, and emerging choices of classroom techniques. Simply put, when a new technique works, we incorporate it into our teaching repertoire; if we perceive that it does not work, we discard it. Often, we do one or the other without considering why the new strategy does or does not resonate with the teaching persona that we built in the classroom.

Harvard professor Sarah Lawrence-Lightfoot says that to substantively understand our teaching we "have to learn to recognize the autobiographical and ancestral roots that run through [our] school lives" (2003, p. 7). Some of the ancestral roots of our professorial practices come not just from our role as "teacher" but also from our role as "student." We each have touchstone stories from our work in graduate school, for instance, about our intellectual and academic ancestors. When new doctoral students come into my office and hint about the lack of confidence they're feeling in those first graduate courses, I find myself often retelling this story about my own graduate school experience.

As an undergraduate student I felt my ignorance made me conspicuous. So much was unfamiliar to me as a shy, first-generation college student. While these feelings were mitigated somewhat with each course and each degree I completed, vestiges of them continued to echo in my head as I enrolled in a doctoral program. Even though I had been recruited by the professor who became my major advisor, I struggled to match my eagerness for advanced studies with the voice in my head that doubted I was up to the intellectual challenge. Shortly after I arrived on campus and got settled in the teaching assistants' office, I decided to confront my insecurities and see what might lie ahead.

Grad School Decision

I approached my doctoral advisor and asked if he would loan me a dissertation because I wanted to see the kind of culminating work I was expected to complete. He obliged by handing me a recently completed dissertation. I went home to read it, worried that my fears that my admittance to the doctoral program had been a sham might be confirmed. They were. It took me hours to work my way through the intimidating document. My attempt to make sense of it confirmed my ignorance. The next morning, I walked sadly to my office and began packing up. I justified my decision to leave by thinking that I would be saving Dr. Davenport and others the arduous task of trying to teach me, and I would save myself from the looming failure. I returned the borrowed dissertation.

After thanking Dr. Davenport I put the dissertation on his desk along with the program withdrawal form. He looked at me with a puzzled expression on this face and asked why I would make such a decision after only a few weeks. I gathered my resolve and explained, "I am not smart enough to be here. I read the entire dissertation, and I didn't understand it." (In my head there was a silent subtext: "Your belief in my potential to do this work was unwarranted.") I pushed the withdrawal paper toward him.

To my surprise he actually chuckled. "I didn't give you the dissertation expecting you to read it all the way through—I don't understand parts of it myself!" He went on to assure me that graduate school was about learning and not about already knowing. He was there, he said, along with my committee members to support my work and growth in my studies. He smiled and said it was likely that if a first-semester doctoral student were to read my own completed dissertation straight through, he or she would probably struggle to understand the work as well. I mentally struggled to balance his words and my fears.

We compromised and I agreed to stay until the end of the withdrawal period. I did stay and complete my coursework and wrote a dissertation. You would think that after all these years I would consider this story a relic of past insecurities, that I might even find some humor in what seems to be an exaggerated reaction to a simple act. But through the years I have learned that no amount of evidence to the contrary assuages those feelings. I have just become better at hiding them.

Even with roughly twenty years between the stories "Winter Saturday Classroom" and "Grad School Decision," I find they share at least a couple of basic themes: the teacher held the power (as a student in the second story, I was metaphorically raising my hand asking for permission to leave the room), the teacher held the answer, and the answer was the key to achievement. The addition of the "Winter Saturday Classroom" story and the "Grad School Decision" story to the story "Kirby's Paper" in the Preface—only three stories from early in my educational biography—gives me a glimpse of the overarching narrative I bring to my teaching. These individual episodes contribute to a larger narrative that has an unacknowledged and unexamined role in my approach to teaching today. Clearly, my educational story has some roots in the "sage on the stage" model.

My reflection on these stories comes first from the stories themselves, then from the details in the retellings, and then from an initial step of analysis. This will not always be an easy or comfortable process, but you will find that it does lead to clarifying insights into themes in your teaching. This book provides a process for undertaking such reflection as a path toward growth. Before pursuing insights from the stories in which we are characters, looking at stories professors "write" as a natural part of their work heightens an awareness of the inherently storied nature of professorial lives. Seeking a deepened understanding of our teaching calls for a "systematic, thoughtful, thorough and objective analysis" (Weimer, 2010, p. 24). One way to undertake this work is to begin with the story-making that is an inherent part of our daily work.

Daily Story-Making

Although I have used some of my own stories to illustrate points in speeches and professional writings over the years, I was unaware of the ways I author stories on a daily basis in my work as a college teacher. This eventual realization opened my eyes to my own authorship of stories that were so close to me that I had not seen them: I painstakingly update my academic story in a curriculum vitae; each semester I outline what is essentially the story of a course in a syllabus; and as a part of my research I try to write clearly and convincingly about my findings and how I arrived at them. Once it occurred to me that I constructed such stories on a regular basis I began to think about my work slightly differently. Without consciously intending to do so, I came to analyze each of the items to see what I could learn. Eventually this led to my realization that the types of stories I wove into my speeches and writings could themselves be sites for analysis. It turned out to be one small step toward my work in scrutinizing such stories rather than just retelling them.

By briefly giving you a glimpse of how you are similarly the author of stories in these areas, you will have an entry point into the ways your work is infused with unacknowledged stories. Whether you are in physics, music, anthropology, nursing, or engineering, for instance, each of you constructs stories in the language of your discipline. Paying attention to these stories may be a new endeavor, but daily story-making is not a wholly unfamiliar activity.

Vita as Story

We are used to taking pains to explicitly tell our academic biography in our curricula vitae. We list degrees obtained, manuscripts published, courses taught, committees served, and honors received. A closer look reveals the locales, the dates, the progression, and the scope of our work. Embedded within vita entries are stories about the professors, institutions, colleagues, students, and circumstances that have contributed to the crafting of our professorial career. Recalling such stories can be a starting point for paying deliberate attention to the autobiographical roots of our teaching practices. There is an entry in my curriculum vitae that says I graduated from Minnesota's Bemidji State College in the late 1960s. That simple entry hides a very significant part of my job history:

Library Firing

I was fired from my work-study job in the college library during undergraduate school. Fired for reading books rather than shelving them. Getting a job in the library meant I had a refuge in the unfamiliar environment of a college campus, and I was eager to prove I deserved to be there. Working in a library was simply the continuation of the hours I had spent in book stacks when I was growing up. The card catalogue and Dewey Decimal System had been guides I used as maps to unexplored worlds. When I began the college library job I worked quickly at returning books to the stacks, but my supervisor had no additional tasks to assign to me when I sought her out. Often she charitably told me to do my homework. I was so thrilled to be working in a library but so disappointed at being told to do the homework that I could do later in my dorm room. After a few weeks of slowing the pace of my work and feeling like I was missing opportunities to learn, I purposefully pushed the book cart into the stacks with a plan: I would read the first paragraph of the books before I returned them to the shelves.

It occurs to me as I write this here that as an eighth grader I had responded similarly to a related experience. After being told I was not allowed to move from the children's to the adult side of the local public library until I was a ninth grader, I vowed to read through the children's fiction section beginning with the books on the top shelf of the A section. As a college student, as I had then, I kept my plan a secret. Now, I no longer went looking for my supervisor—she came looking for me. Instead of my asking her for more work, her mission was to ask me for more work.

This cycle repeated itself three or four times. I would go back to doing the job too quickly, then I would get frustrated enough to return to my surreptitious reading. Eventually, she found me sitting on the floor in the stacks, interrupted my reading, and told me my services were no longer needed. Embarrassed and shame-faced, I went back to the financial aid officer who had placed me in that job and confessed to both my firing from the job and my secretive reading. He listened to my library story, and with one phone call he was able to place me in a position as the student assistant to the English Department chairperson.

Within the last decade I have retold this "Library Firing" story a dozen times, often after someone has introduced me to a group by referring to some entries on my vita. In my acknowledgment of the generosity of my host, I point out that my curriculum vitae (a phrase derived from Latin and roughly meaning "the course of my life") *should* more honestly include entries such as:

1957—home-school teacher, Hibbing, Minnesota

1968—fired from college library position, Bemidji State College

1979—student of Dr. Davenport, Arizona State University

Even though these three incidents are not explicitly listed in my vita, they inhabit it. Poet Demetria Martínez titles one of her books *Breathing Between the Lines* (1997). Our stories live between the lines of our academic accomplishments even after the experiences that gave rise to the stories are years past.

> I invite you to give some thought to a few of the stories that live be-
> tween the lines of your own vita. Consider people or circumstances
> that are invisible entries in your academic account. This might provide
> the impetus to share the anecdotes with one or more others, to jot
> down a few notes, or just to spend a few moments recalling the inci-
> dents. Use this opportunity to draw on your own curriculum vitae to
> illustrate to yourself how stories are integral to your formal biography.

A curriculum vitae is only one example of the way that our academic lives are, in fact, lives of everyday story-making.

Syllabus as Story

We walk into the first day of a semester's class with syllabus in hand, and we are prepared to explain to students how they will be characters in the story of a course called, for instance, American History. It is unlikely that we have ever thought about a syllabus as containing features of a story. In literature, stories are said to have seven common elements: character, plot, setting, theme, tone, style, and point of view. Even in classes far removed from literature, such as courses in political science, calculus, biology, or art, these elements of stories are a part of how we structure our courses. I do not intend to convince you that this is so, but to provide you with two examples and an opportunity to consider the presence of some of these elements in your own discipline-based course planning.

In thinking about it this way, consider the plot of a course entitled "Alexander Solzhenitsyn's Literature and Politics" I team-taught years ago with a political science professor. We constructed the course around the question, "Was the Nobel Prize in Literature awarded to Solzhenitsyn primarily for his literary contributions or his political stance?" A variation of this "plot" summary appeared in the course catalogue. The "setting" of the story involved two professors from different disciplines and a class of undergraduates meeting in the social science building one day a week for sixteen weeks from 2:00 pm to 5:00 pm. The story's "theme": "Some seemingly settled matters are open to productive debate." These elements (character, plot, setting, theme) were explicitly present in our syllabus although not labeled as such. Three additional elements (tone, style, and point of view) were also implicitly present in the syllabus and modeled in our first class session. My colleague and I set a "tone" of respectful disagreement in the way we conducted the first class, we communicated a dialogic "style," and we each brought a "point of view" to our introduction of the content.

I invite you to consider a course you teach now or have in the past. The elements of story may be more evident to you in a course you have developed yourself. Think about how one or more of the seven narrative elements play a role in how your course is framed. Which of the elements of story are evident in your syllabus? What additional elements are evident in the way you introduce the syllabus and conduct class?

Throughout the semester, students build their own stories of the courses they take. Their class participation, exam performance, assignment responses, and office-hour visits may have us revising the story we outline in the syllabus. While we do not think about this explicitly, those revisions mean that students become coauthors.

Students Asked Me to Leave

I distributed the carefully constructed syllabus to the juniors on the first day of English 335, "Methods of Teaching Language," in which the theme of the semester was that "Language studies are integral to teaching English." I wanted to know what background students brought to the study because I was never certain they were as prepared as they should be. Once the students each introduced themselves, I asked them to complete a prior-knowledge quiz as a preface to our study. The results would give me an idea of the extent to which they had the background necessary to proceed or if I needed to extend the introductory material to remediate their insufficient preparation. Class concluded, they dutifully filed out, and I collected the papers they had left piled on the desk.

By using item analysis, I was able to assess the quizzes and give each student a score in five categories of grammatical knowledge. When I used that data to plot a class profile, it was clear to me that in those areas where some were the strongest, others were the weakest. I walked into the next class period a bit frustrated about needing to adjust my introductory plans once again and review key aspects covered by the pretest.

When I arrived, someone who had obviously been appointed as class spokesperson raised their hand. The student said that given my first-day-of-class explanation of how we would go over any areas of deficiency that surfaced in their prior-knowledge quiz, they had an alternate plan. I was surprised they assumed my plan would need to be altered. The spokesperson explained that they wanted me to stay in my office for the next two class periods instead of coming to class so that they could teach each other. This was only the second class meeting.

I was speechless. I had deliberately orchestrated the opening class meetings and doubted any students were in a position to make changes. Students said they wanted me to stay in my office during those class periods so they could come by if they had any questions while they were working with each other. I did not trust them, but for reasons I can't explain other than a perverse need to prove my view was warranted, I hesitatingly agreed. They were, I thought, presuming an expertise I did not imagine they had.

Once I distributed the results of the quiz, they used their scores in the five categories to pair up people with apparent mastery in some areas with those with apparent deficiencies. As they did this, I admit that I felt my position in the class had been usurped. I reluctantly scheduled the next two class periods as office hours. My consultation hours turned out to be exactly that. Pairs of students came in for short tutoring sessions, only to return to the classroom to work with their colleagues. I was surprised by the seriousness of their questions and their demeanor. I did, however, feel like I was in some way being held hostage.

A class representative came in and asked me to give the same quiz when I returned to class as a way for them to gauge their progress. When I did return for the retest, an analysis of the results showed that most students demonstrated growth in at least one area. With their actions they had rewritten part of my syllabus: they coauthored the opening chapter of "Methods of Teaching English" in ways that I would not have imagined. They re-scripted my lines. They revised the plot. They shifted the tone. I did not realize it at the time but I have come to see since that my teaching benefited from their teaching, even though I was not yet ready for it.

The storied nature of the course syllabus and the brief, memorable moments it gives rise to illustrate how stories live in our professional work. In her Nobel Prize acceptance lecture, writer and Nobel laureate Toni Morrison said, "Narrative is radical, creating us at the very moment it is being created" (1994, p. 27). This classroom narrative, "Students Asked Me to Leave," is a convergence of daily stories—the students', mine as their teacher, and the story of the content. At the same time that this little plot was unfolding, our understanding of our roles (how we each "played school") was being created. In this story, faculty and students contributed to making these stories and were simultaneously being made by them.

In the same way that my students built a collective story in English 335, they bring their individual stories into class with them. It can be easier for us to be aware of their stories than it is to be fully aware of our own. In many cases we are in a position to decide on the efficacy of students' stories and then to decide on a response.

No matter how we interact with the stories that students bring to teachers, we get glimpses into their lives:

"I missed class because I had to go to the health center."

"My paper is late because I had to work a double shift."

"I wasn't prepared for lab because my computer crashed."

The range of stories that we hear is rich and varied. Our daily lives are full of the mundane, the mindful, the comedic, and the dramatic in our classrooms. In *My Freshman Year: What a College Professor Learned by Being a Student* (2005), author Rebekah Nathan enrolled as a freshman at Any U, lived in the dorm, and took a schedule of undergraduate classes. In a section of the book where she reflects back on lessons that she learned during that year ("Lessons from My Year as a Freshman," pp. 132–156), Dr. Nathan describes a story that has stayed with her:

> I had observed students managing their identities, placating their parents, positioning their future, and finding their place in peer circles. I can vividly remember overhearing the authentic excitement in one student's voice when she exclaimed into her cell phone, "Mom, the professor told me the essay was really good!" I keep that image of what is on the other end of a professor's encouragement. (p. 134)

Nathan's work illustrates how students' stories intersect with and influence our own. When Kirby came to my office to contest an essay grade ("Kirby's Paper," in the Preface), we ended up revising each other's stories. In "Students Asked Me to Leave," the revision meant the syllabus was altered as were we. In our professional writing, we also develop a type of story that aims to inform—even alter—the thinking of others.

Professional Writing

Scholarly writing that describes research findings for peer review contains elements of stories. Considering this can provide additional insights into the kaleidoscopic nature of the way our professional narrative is framed by major documents in our professional lives. In April of 1994, an award-winning novelist visited our campus. In his address to the faculty, he sketched out the similarities between story development and the development of our scholarly essays. He said that in reporting on our research we seek to make believers out of our readers. Although the material we use in the scholarly essays is different from what he puts into his novels, there are, he explained, parallels in the processes. In scholarly manuscripts we review historical material (he said in his fiction he used such historical elements poetically); in both types of writing we have "a duty to testify to what we see and feel"; we write details that resonate with a theme; and we use details to illuminate both a "plot" (or line of thinking) and a "theme" (the point of that thinking). The vitae, syllabi, and professional writing are three types of stories that are at the marrow of our professorial lives even when we haven't thought of them in this way before.

Shifting the Contextual Frames

The university context in which this work is accomplished itself has a story. University mission statements and strategic plans circumscribe the details of our work. The university's approach to teaching in an even broader context can influence our local approach—our story-building. As I began to sense changes in how I was thinking about my teaching within these two contexts I came across a book describing this process: *Frame Reflection: Toward the Resolution of Intractable Policy Controversies* (Schön and Rein, 1994). Schön's earlier books (*The Reflective Practitioner: How Professionals Think in Action*, 1983, and *Educating the Reflective Practitioner*, 1987) were interesting to me, but *Frame Reflection* helped me in the initial steps of seeing that there might be some overarching themes in my own stories about my teaching. Although Schön and Rein were writing about the public policy arena, their concept of frame reflection I felt had merit for the field of higher education as it relates to teaching.

"[F]rames," they write, are tacit "underlying structures of belief, perception, and appreciation" (p. 23). From the beginning of my teaching in the "Winter Saturday Classroom," my experiences led to an ongoing reinforcement of certain "underlying structures of belief" about my role as a teacher. Before reflecting on our own professional "frames" in subsequent chapters, looking at how the concept is at work in university contexts can inform that exploration.

The literature about teaching at colleges is regularly framed in two ways: "instruction-centered" and "learner-centered." At the beginning of a book by John Tagg called *The Learning Paradigm College* (2003) in which he proposes that we shift from the first frame to the latter, Tagg opens with a personal story that illustrates what happens when major shifts occur—he recounts his experience as a young boy who finds out that he needs glasses. When he put on the new glasses, his view of the world suddenly and dramatically changed. In place of fuzzy shapes and muted colors, he saw vivid colors, sharp lines, and an "abundance of pattern, of complexity" (p. 3). Now, years later, this story is featured prominently at the beginning of his book which describes a new context through which institutions view their work; as he says in the concluding sentences of this opening story, "New lenses changed everything. And that was not a metaphor or a hyperbole. They really did change everything" (p. 3). Seeing how a new lens brings a changed view to the university context of teaching provided me with insights into my own work.

An earlier and influential essay was written by Tagg with colleague Robert Barr (1995) that called on universities to rethink the lens—the frame—that as institutions they bring to teaching and learning. In order to contrast two frameworks for learning in higher education they lay out columns pairing the two different views. With the first view, the "instruction-centered" lens, they discuss what they observed was the relationship between teaching and learning most evident at the time. The features that they list as illustrative of this instruction-centered paradigm are reminiscent of Charles Dickens's parody of the professor in *Hard Times* ([1854] 2007). Dickens's Professor Thomas Gradgrind gave facts and asked students to recite what he presented. My expectations in "Winter Saturday Classroom" and "Students Asked Me to Leave" were similar. Barr and Tagg have a comprehensive list of over three dozen characteristics of what they saw as evidence of the prominence of this instruction-centered paradigm. As I read their essay I found they were describing some elements that had become calcified in my teaching through the earliest years and therefore presented me with a serious challenge when I sought to shift my thinking. Among the characteristics Barr and Tagg cite illustrating this frame are the following:

The instruction-centered paradigm is one in which

- "Transfer knowledge [moves from] faculty to students"

- There is a focus on "inputs"

- "[K]nowledge comes in chunks and bits; [and is] delivered by instructors and gotten by students"

From my vantage point now as someone who is reflecting on formative stories in my educational biography, it is hard to read this brief excerpt from their list because its resonance with my earlier views on the nature of teaching is unsettling. Today, I envision myself as someone whose teaching-frame springs from different assumptions, but through the examination of critical incidents in my teaching I have also learned that features of this instruction-centered frame continue to influence my work.

To contrast the second frame, the learner-centered paradigm, Barr and Tagg place contrasting characteristics across from each other in a two-column list. The features included below illustrate a trio of points that parallel and contrast with the points listed above.

The learner-centered paradigm is one in which

- Teachers "elicit students' discovery and construction of knowledge"

- There is a focus on "learning and student success outcomes"

- "[K]nowledge exists in each person's mind and is shaped by individual experience"

In describing the profound nature of these contrasting views, Barr and Tagg essentially demonstrate the point of Tagg's story about his getting new glasses: "This new lens changes everything" (2003, p. 3). In a pared-down form, the frame that has governed colleges is this: A college is an institution that aims to *provide instruction*. Subtly but profoundly we are shifting to a new paradigm: A college is an institution that aims to *produce learning*. This institutional shift is an evolutionary one. So is the glacial change in my teaching as I seek to use stories to understand its characteristics.

In 2002, Maryellen Weimer's *Learner-Centered Teaching: Five Key Changes to Practice* brought the institutional focus of the Barr and Tagg essay into the classroom. She posited that there are five keys to consider in making the shift from instruction-centered to learner-centered pedagogy: (1) balance of power, (2) function of content, (3) role of the teacher, (4) responsibility for learning, and (5) the purposes and processes of evaluation. This is useful because it names components of the lenses and addresses what the shift looks like within the college classroom. My initial teaching experience as a ten-year-old in Northern Minnesota illustrates something about the distant roots of my beliefs about teaching: I confidently knew what I was doing; I was charged with keeping my siblings quiet, occupied, and under control until it was time for their afternoon naps. It never occurred to me that there was any other option. I was enthralled with the power of my position. Of course, I could always threaten to report my sisters and brother to our parents if they got so far out of line that swatting them with damp mittens did not work. It did not occur to me that there was any other way to "see" the situation.

For me, the "Five Keys to Change" Weimer writes about were all stuck in a proverbial lock: there was no balance of power, my own expertise determined the content, my role was an authoritarian one, I demanded they memorize their math combinations, and when they took the afternoon tests, they got red marks on their paper signaling how poorly they had done. There was no such thing as "frame reflection." The winters in Hibbing were so long that there were endless opportunities for me to practice and reinforce my approach. Because this approach was also reinforced by teachers I had over the years, it is no surprise that reflecting on my pedagogical frame is difficult work for me to tackle. The same may be true for you as we work through an identification and analysis of your key stories in this book.

As I have worked to understand what underlying structures frame my teaching, I have also been diligent over the years in my reading of the pedagogical literature. In trying to incorporate this sweep of literature into my growth, however, I sometimes find myself feeling like Al, a character in Wallace Stegner's Angle of Repose (1971). Al's poor vision means that he has to wear quadruple-focal glasses. Given that he owns a Laundromat, Al has to fix the machines by sticking his head into the washers: "'Ever try to thee with your head inthide a Bendix?" Al asks with a lisp. His friend replies, 'I get the message. Space being curved, tunnel vision and the rigid neck could leave a man focused on the back of his own head'" (p. 77). I can relate to Al's predicament.

When I told the story "Students Asked Me to Leave" earlier in this chapter I did not include a next step that I took. As a consequence of the students' change of the course context, I gave deliberate thought to the value of the resulting students' claim to teaching themselves. It was not entirely comfortable to look closely at my teaching and think about the challenge they issued to me. In time, I hesitatingly tried some group work with varied results—small steps of growth. The calls for more "reflective practitioners" (Schön, 1983, 1987; Brookfield, 1995) are calls for personal growth in understanding the dimensions of one's teaching.

When we are prompted to try something new in one of our classes—like I did in agreeing to leave the classroom in the hands of students, no matter how reluctantly—we also have the potential of moving into the realm of reflective teaching. In doing so we initially engage in what Argyris and Schön discuss as "single-loop learning" (1974). That was me: with this "single-loop learning" the emphasis is on "techniques and making techniques more efficient"" (Usher and Bryant in Smith, 2001).

In a call for more substantive attention to one's professional frames, Argyris and Schön (1974) describe the power of "double-loop learning." Double-loop learning is the process I'm engaging in as the book proceeds. It is more complicated because it involves bringing questions to the very use and consequences of the teaching techniques we choose: "Reflection here is more fundamental: the basic assumptions behind ideas or policies are confronted ..." (Smith, 2001). In *Becoming a Critically Reflective Teacher* (1995), Brookfield calls on us to go "assumption hunting" (p. 3)—to practice double-loop learning.

On occasion, I have led teaching workshops that in turn have encouraged colleagues to try some of the practices that have worked particularly well for professors who write or speak about them. I have distributed Bain's book *What the Best College Teachers Do* (2004), for instance, so that attendees can look at a variety of teaching practices implemented across the disciplines. Leading and attending such sessions are not unproductive, but the question is, how do we extend this single-loop learning and take up the riskier double-loop learning? How can we become a more reflective teacher so "best practices" come to be personally grounded and resonant with our aspirations?

"Critical reflection," "frame reflection," "single-loop learning," "double-loop learning," "instruction-centered and learner-centered paradigms"—I do not include the concepts here to make you feel like you are wearing quadruple-focal glasses like Al in *Angle of Repose*; I include them because each of these concepts informs our understanding of institutional contexts and the contexts of the process of reflection. As I made my way through the literature spanning my career, doing so incrementally affected how I looked at my teaching. But it was an eventual awareness and then scrutiny of my stories that moved me from being an observer to being a participant in this shift. Some stories persist, and coming to know *how* and *why* can help us move from single-loop learning to double-loop learning (Argyris and Schön, 1974), from knowledge-in-action to reflection-on-action (Schön, 1983), and from reflection to critical reflection (Weimer, 2010).

Next Steps

Among the questions posed in the Preface are these three: "I wonder what stories have accompanied you along the way?" "What stories reappear as you recall or possibly retell them?" "I wonder what it is about the incidents that keep certain stories within reach?" While my own stories have been folded into the exploration of frameworks in this chapter, Chapter Two invites you to begin work with recalling those stories in your own repertoire. Your former students, grad college professors, or fifth grade teachers may rise to the surface as you are prompted to take an inventory of incidents that come back to you when they are purposefully pursued. I expect you will, like I have, find some joy in bringing these stories back into your life. I have also found a host of other emotions but have learned through the process laid out in subsequent chapters that there is a collective richness in the stories. In his article "Pedagogy, Virtue, and Narrative Identity in Teaching," Max van Manen says, "Personal identity can be brought to self-awareness through narrative self-reflection" (1994, p. 159). Stories live in our teaching beyond the moments in which they occur.

2

Living Stories

In all classrooms, even in the hard sciences, professors use stories, usually in the form of anecdotes, to illustrate points, to elucidate information that may be abstract. Story, especially personal story, is one of the most powerful ways to educate.

(hooks, 2010, p. 56)

O ne of my colleagues in the Department of Geology teaches an undergraduate general education course, "Geologic Disasters." On a day when I visited her class, she was reviewing the students' reading assignment on the processes that affect land surface and land formations. After she showed some photographs of the phenomenon, she moved into a brief personal story. She had recently purchased land for a house. In order to decide where to put the foundation, she explained, she had to look at all of the land features to determine the safest place for the house, including its septic tank and the drain field. "I used the very information we are reading about to help me make the decisions."

In addition to the ways discussed in Chapter One that stories are built into our curricula vitae, our course syllabi, professional writing, and the context of our work, this simple example from geology class illustrates how two additional types of stories are infused into each class period we teach. I was introduced to these types of stories when I read researcher Sigrun Gudmundsdottir's insights (1991). She helped me realize that narratives traverse our classes. I briefly introduce her work here to augment the work in Chapter One and to lead to the initial identification of personal stories that undergird your teaching.

Within each class and within each course there are, Gudmundsdottir explains, two ways that we build stories into classroom teaching: what she calls the *story-making* dimension and the *story-telling* dimension (p. 208). The story-*making* dimension is what we engage in prior to teaching course material as we make decisions about what content will constitute the study. Through the selection and organization of content, a story is "made." The other dimension, the story-*telling* dimension, is where we tell stories to illustrate key points that relate to those that were selected for study. "Textbooks tell stories and teachers bring stories to tell" (Gudmundsdottir, 1991, p. 213).

To illustrate Gudmundsdottir's two ideas, consider how my colleague teaches her introductory course. In her planning, she selects the facts and concepts from the required textbook that will form the content. The topics that she lists in her syllabus range from volcanoes and earthquakes to floods and landslides. She thus engages in the "story-making" dimension. To teach relying only on this dimension, however, is likely to do little to engage students in understanding the material.

In addition to drawing a course storyline from reference materials and texts, this geology instructor does what most faculty do as they teach: She finds ways to bring the content to life by combining it with examples, local references, and even metaphors. Class becomes the site of "story-telling." My colleague weaves in the types of details that invite students to see their environment in newly informed ways. For instance, she tells about taking the two-and-a-half-hour road trip from the mountain city of Flagstaff, at an elevation of 7,000 feet, to the desert floor in Phoenix. When she drives this route, she explains, she sees the land features as more than points on a map; as she descends, she sees the story of the evolution of the land features preserved in the rocks. She asks students to do the same on their next trip to the Valley so that they can combine the course content with stories of their own.

Each of these two dimensions, the "story-making" and the "story-telling," illuminates the other. Through this geology instructor's use of personal examples and local references, the geologic origins of Flagstaff's San Francisco Peaks makes clearer the content about the volcanic process, and her fact-based description of rock formation makes the sight of the red rocks of Sedona more meaningful. Simultaneous to *her* story-making and story-telling, students are similarly engaged in both dimensions. They engage in their own story-making as they highlight passages in the readings they've selected as significant and as they take notes on the material in the lectures. The further the students get into a semester, the better able they are to also move into story-telling where they can take examples from their own lives and talk in class about related personal experiences that link to the content. The classroom, whether lecture hall or seminar room, is full of stories being acknowledged and constructed.

Chapter One illustrated the ways in which stories are omnipresent in our lives as college professors in the professional contexts that frame our work. By becoming aware of these storied aspects of being a college teacher, the role of "story-building" (a combination of both of Gudmundsdottir's dimensions) can be recognized for the way it is woven into our professional lives. With this increased awareness of the integral presence of stories, uncovering assumptions shaped by those stories becomes possible. This possibility is enhanced by our turning to stories within our own educational biographies.

Storied Foundations

We come to college teaching with a near lifelong career as students having moved through elementary, secondary, and multiple layers of postsecondary education. This history provides enough familiarity with the classrooms for us to be critics of teaching. As students in a succession of settings, we know what reached us, what distanced us, what engaged us, and what influenced us in positive and less-than-positive ways. Examples in Chapter One and the beginning of Chapter Two point to the ubiquitous nature of stories that may not be recognized as such. Now, this chapter pursues a recollection of the stories that live in our memories beyond how a syllabus is constructed or how a class is conducted.

School stories from our educational biographies have an often unacknowledged influence on our educational practices (Lawrence-Lightfoot, 2003, p. 7). When the gaze shifts from stories we construct while teaching to the stories we bring to that teaching, it becomes possible to locate some of our underlying influences. English professor Jane Tompkins wrote about her own "exploratory mission" in A Life in School: What a Teacher Learned (1996), which began with the acknowledgment that "I had been molded as a teacher by the teachers who had molded me" (p. xvi). Such an understanding is not as straightforward as it may seem because reconsidering and then untangling interconnected stories only begins with recalling them.

In considering how different it feels to pay careful, deliberate attention to stories we might initially see as interesting or entertaining anecdotes, it is useful to try a little experiment:

> Before reading further, take a piece of paper and write your first and last name using your nondominant hand. Doing this will illustrate the next point.

Think about how you approached and responded to this strange task—a task that appears to be unrelated to the topic of this book. Did you begin immediately? Did you try to visualize your name written in the usual way before you began proceeding backwards? Did you move more slowly through the task, more deliberately than when not faced with those directions? Did you bring more conscious attention to each step? Was there any degree of automaticity?

Identifying stories and then moving through the three stages of reflection in this book is not unlike this task of writing your name with your nondominant hand: the process is unusual, slow, deliberate, and unexpected. Instead of pulling individual stories from memories to retell in times of appropriate promptings (as in my Chapter One response to a question asked by an airplane seatmate), using stories from educational biographies as a basis for reflection involves reconsidering memories in a different way. And it is the subsequent scrutiny of key stories that echoes the experience of seeing your name written in an unanticipated way.

Using stories in the service of undertaking critical reflection on teaching begins with remembering the stories from our lives as students in other people's classrooms. When prompted to recall an incident from my years as a student, the memory of Miss Hentges's approach to recognizing students as individuals comes to mind. On its surface, what follows is a simple story about a simple response to a simple problem:

Miss Hentges's Recognition

Fifth grade was an eye-opener. In the mid-1950s there were, as there are today, popular names for children, which meant that classes could have more than one pupil with the same first name. "Linda" was one of those names then. During the first few weeks of school I felt lost in a sea of girls named "Linda." Miss Hentges would call out that name, and then I would wait to see if I was the one who would be singled out by her steely gaze. I recall even now that I felt a bit under water in her classroom; I could hide in the sea of other Lindas, but longed to be recognized for my individual identity. Miss Hentges surprised me. One day she came in with her seating chart and looked at Linda Griffin and called her "Linda G," then looked at Linda Frances and called her

"Linda F," and then eventually asked me a question after addressing me as "Linda C." With this small act of acknowledgment, I can still feel how my confidence level rose. The words in the primer seemed more manageable, the spelling tests less daunting, and her gaze seemed to soften.

Something about this story lives on in the metaphorical audio-tape that accompanies my life. It is a story that I have retold to fellow students at a class reunion, a story that I have previously written about (Shadiow, 1985), and a story that almost six decades later I find myself retelling here. The longer this story has been with me, the more I have come to realize that its meaning has evolved. I think Miss Hentges, for instance, was in part behind the affinity I felt when I first read philosopher Charles Taylor's work on the politics of recognition (1992). His work discusses how the ways we have of recognizing people (and ourselves being recognized) are imbued with power dynamics. Through multiple stages of reflection I have come to learn about just such a legacy with the story "Miss Hentges's Recognition." It is part of what led me to examine the very practices I brought to recognizing and establishing relationships with students in my classrooms where I was teaching. I was better able to ask myself, "What does it mean to acknowledge people in different ways?" As we move through the process in this book together, some of your own stories will take on deepened meaning as you approach them using a series of reflective lenses.

In recalling and noting identifying details of your own stories, you might begin with those stories that come easily to mind when you are reading the stories included in this book. Using the familiar language of lived experiences is an early stage of collecting "data" for this book's project on reflection. There will be three prompts to focus your collection of stories. By the conclusion of this chapter you will have been prompted to recall incidents from three different contexts. The first of these contexts is, like my "Miss Hentges's

Recognition," set in other people's classrooms where you have been a student.

Being a Student

To begin the process of critical reflection on your own work as a college professor, take a moment to reminisce about your years as a student. Using Tompkins's phrase, consider this as the beginning of an "exploratory mission." Some stories may come immediately to mind or this may take some time; you may find such a flood of stories that you have little difficulty identifying some or you may only be able to remember one or two—take a break and give yourself time to identify others. In either case, let your mind play with the idea of reminiscence; picture classrooms, teachers, administrators, counselors, and teachers' aides and see, with some purposeful attention to your memories, what you remember.

I invite you to begin:

Think back on your life as a student; consider elementary, secondary, and college experiences. Recall at least three stories from your school life that are memorable enough to come to mind. They may have been positive (like my story of Miss Hentges) or not. Write down a few identifying phrases to bring each incident into focus. Through these brief phrases highlight major details that distinguish one story from another (e.g., "Miss Hentges; fifth grade; many Lindas"). The stories recalled in this chapter will become the basis for taking a closer look at details beginning in Chapter Three. What are three stories that come to mind when you think about your life as a student?

Memories like these from our educational biographies provide the beginnings of a narrative landscape, and "To be in touch with our landscapes is to be ... aware of the ways we encounter the world" (Greene, 1978, p. 2). Even if our memories as students spring from a range of classroom and school contexts, the features of the landscape that Greene discusses can be discovered. Stories can, for instance, form motifs that underpin directions we have taken in our lives. Whether we are unaware of these motifs like I was with the "politics of recognition" in Miss Hentges's classroom or vividly conscious of influential connections through the years like in the story that follows, looking into the stories can help us learn about how we "encounter the world."

Prominent educator Ernest Boyer, the former president of the Carnegie Foundation for the Advancement of Teaching, recounted the following story about a time in his early schooling when a teacher made an impact. Boyer repeatedly used the story to make a point about the significant roles teachers play in the lives of students. I heard him tell this story on two different occasions, and I paraphrase it here:

Young Ernest Boyer was accompanied by his mother as he walked to school on his first day. She held his hand as they crossed the street and talked about the day ahead. "What do you think you will learn in school today?" she asked. He remembers looking up at her and confidently making this announcement: "Today I'm going to learn how to read." She gently responded by telling him that learning to read is a difficult job that takes hard work and a great deal of time.

When they arrived at school, a woman standing outside young Ernie's classroom welcomed students and parents. After he was seated at his desk and after all the desks were occupied, the same woman "floated into the room as if on a cloud." In a book of published speeches Boyer explains what happened next. She surveyed the room of "twenty-eight frightened, awestruck, anticipating children, 'Good morning, class. Today we learn to read'" (Boyer, 1997, p. 77).

I remember Boyer saying that the class spent the day looking at words on the blackboard and reciting, "My name is . . ." as she pointed to the collection of words. Then they copied the hieroglyphics onto sheets of lined paper. Eventually the teacher distributed a specially prepared paper to each student, and Ernie worked on his by carefully tracing over the words, "My name is Ernest Boyer."

When his mother picked him up at the end of the day she asked, "What did you learn in school today?" He reached into his pocket and carefully unfolded a piece of paper. He said, "Today I learned how to read." Then I recall that he explained that he proceeded to stare at the words on the paper and haltingly recited, "My. name. is. Ernest. Boyer."

This memory was woven through the tapestry of reasons for why he chose a career in education and later made the decision to pursue educational administration. Eventually, he moved into the position of Chancellor of the State University of New York, then to U.S. Commissioner of Education, and later, to the position of President of the Carnegie Foundation for the Advancement of Teaching, a policy and research center aimed at reforming education. This story was told in a series of speeches he made when he was asked to address the ways that the educational landscape *could* be. Years after the incident, Boyer's multiple tellings of the story point not just to its resilience but to the influence of its themes. The first three stories you noted were drawn from those like Boyer's, stories from days of being a student.

Being a Teacher

Equally as powerful as stories linked to our days as students are stories linked to our lives as teachers. These are the stories we tell colleagues in the hallways and to our family and friends. I have told three of these stories—in the Preface, "Kirby's Paper," and in Chapter One, "Winter Saturday Classroom" and "Students Asked Me to Leave." I find each one grows in meaning and significance as the years pass. There is much in doing this work on reflection that surprises me, and the changing nature of the stories was among my first insights. In order to explore that dimension in your stories, identify a second set of incidents you recall from your own teaching. For some of us the earliest years in our careers are most vivid because we were new to our work and every experience left an impression. Drawing from the scope of your career as a teacher, whether it began with playing school as a child or is far more recent, identify a second trio of stories to join the first one. In recalling those stories, the accuracy of the facts may seem harder to remember than the story (plot) itself. Rather than let that be an impediment to this process, consider MacDonald's point (2008): "What happened—the facts—are not even as important to empowerment and transformation as the telling of what we remember and how we remember it" (p. 78).

I invite you to continue to draw on incidents from your educational biography:

> Think back on your life as a teacher in either formal classroom settings or informal settings—in either case, times when you and learners interacted. Recall at least three incidents that have had an impact on you. It could be a moment inside or outside a classroom, an exchange with a single student, or an incident involving an entire class. Write down a few identifying phrases to bring each story into focus. What teaching-related incidents come to mind when you think about your career as a teacher?

Among these stories there may have been some particularly significant experiences you have had about something unexpected at the time. One of these moments for me was when I implemented a very simple teaching technique a colleague had passed on to me—waiting five seconds for students to respond to a question rather than jumping in to call on students or answer the questions myself. It was an application of Mary Budd Rowe's work on "wait-time" (1972).

Using Wait-time

I was teaching an upper-division literature class, "Women and Madness," where we were studying works of writers like Sylvia Plath, Anne Sexton, and Zelda Fitzgerald. My modus operandi in the class with about sixty students was to enthusiastically come into class armed with a series of questions to spark what I hoped would be a lively discussion. Much to my dismay, I repeatedly found that I was answering most of the questions myself, and the sixty students were taking notes without being as involved as I had anticipated. I was disappointed in myself because I had always been told that a teacher's enthusiasm for the subject was a prerequisite for engaging students.

During this semester a colleague who taught physics introduced me to a bit of research he said had a profound impact on his teaching. He explained the work this way: Wait-time is the amount of time between when a faculty member asks a question and the time when, if no students respond, the faculty member answers the question him- or herself, calls on a student, asks another question, or moves on. Rowe's research revealed that the average "wait-time" was around one second. In one second, a faculty member expects students to internalize a question, consider alternative responses, select the best alternative, and overcome any reluctance to raise a hand. A daunting set of tasks.

I had a flash of the fevered pace that I used in supposedly prompting class discussions. The reflection on my own teaching was both eye-opening and painfully vivid. I walked into the next class and introduced the focus of the class period and then posed one initial question. I waited, silently counting out five seconds. Students looked up from their notes. I imagined that they wondered if something had happened to me. Instead of racing ahead with my barrage of questions, I waited. A student timidly raised a hand and seemed ready to pull it back down if I opened my mouth. But given my silence, the student responded. After the student spoke, I silently counted out another three seconds (a further recommendation from the research), and the student added more information. Three more seconds and then another student responded. Eventually, a lively discussion was taking place without my constant intervention. I was so used to being the only contributor in class that at one point, I have to admit, I felt left out. It was not easy to break my habit of posing multiple questions and giving answers with barely a breath in between, but over the rest of the semester the definition of "class discussion" in our course changed dramatically enough to still remember it thirty years later.

The effects of this "Using Wait-time" story accompany me into each class I teach. It has helped me understand my classroom decision making, and this means it is more than a story about the implementation of a technique. In combination with an analysis of other stories, I began to see patterns developing in my assumptions about the roles of students, faculty, and content. After identifying a cache of stories, we will work together to prioritize those stories that are "critical incidents." Following that there will be additional steps leading to an exploration of assumptions. Each story in your developing repertoire is, in preliminary ways, an overall part of the framework that will enable this exploration of what Pinar calls "the architecture of self" (1988, p. 27)—the teaching self.

Why do I recommend you start with three stories for each prompt, not one, two, or four? Recalling a single story is easy; they come to mind when prompted by an inquiry or similar incident. Even two stories may rise quickly from our memories because they have made an enduring impression. However, recalling three incidents requires moving further into memories that, while they may be equally as vivid, are in layers that are not as easily recalled. So, the number is somewhat arbitrary. If four or even five memories in one of these areas emerge, the subsequent analysis will be richer for it. If there are fewer than three, the analysis will be less satisfying. For however many stories you have noted so far, one of the results of doing so is an illustration of what Gunn (1982) posits: "The autobiographical perspective has ... to do with bringing oneself to language" (p. 16). In addition to the two groups of stories you have recalled thus far in the chapter, there is one additional trio of stories to "bring to language" before pursuing the initiation of analysis and reflection.

In the Profession

I chose to be a university professor in large part because I could continue to work full-time as a student with unending opportunities for learning. It has only rarely seemed like "work." In addition to the memories of stories from when I was a student learning in someone else's classroom and those from my own experiences in classrooms where I have taught, I have pivotal memories of learning within the broader context of my professional life—at conferences, in research, in books, and from colleagues. Within this professional arena, there have been a number of occasions of significant yet unexpected growth. Here lies a third context for stories that have influenced my professional development.

The impact of the following incident on me will be clearer to you if you think about a preeminent theoretician in your discipline, someone whose work has had an incalculable impact on your field. When the opportunity arose for me to participate in a small conference keynoted by just such a renowned speaker, Brazilian educator Paulo Freire, the resulting experience was beyond anything I could have ever imagined.

Freire has been a foundational figure in educational theory and practice during his life and since his death in 1997. His book, *Pedagogy of the Oppressed* (originally published in Portuguese in 1968), was groundbreaking, as it placed education at the confluence of the presence of authority, power, and colonization but also as a site where freedom can be vigorously pursued. When people speak about the view that education rests on the "banking concept" where students are viewed as empty containers to be filled by prescribed knowledge, they are drawing on Freirean contributions. His work is required reading in college of education graduate classes, as well as both in the classes I took and those I teach.

Bringing Questions to Freire

When it was announced that he would be the featured speaker at the 1992 international SIETAR conference (Society for Intercultural Education, Training, and Research), the prospect of listening to him in person led a colleague and I to submit a paper on how we were applying his theories in our work. When the conference invitation came, I enthusiastically went to a graduate class that I was teaching in curriculum theory to share the news, and I invited students to develop a set of questions that they would like me to ask Freire should the occasion arise. Naively I slipped their questions into my briefcase along with the conference paper. Ironically (given his theories), I went to the conference with the full expectation that he would deposit new knowledge into my empty head. I was a poster child for his critique of learning as a "banking" enterprise.

On the evening of Freire's keynote speech I arrived early to get a front-row seat. I took notes almost nonstop and got down as many direct quotes as I could throughout his address. I scribbled my notes on the blank pages at the front of one of his books, and I have that book in front of me as I write this. After the speech Freire's translator (whom I had been sitting next to) acknowledged my note taking and asked if I would like to meet him. I am sure my facial expression said "yes" before I found a voice to speak. Once the crowd cleared, we went up for introductions. Freire and I shook hands, and he asked what I did. After briefly explaining my work, I mentioned the graduate students and the fact that they had collaborated on a small set of questions for him. He graciously offered to respond to a few. It was clear that he was tired, so after a few of the questions, I thanked him. He said he would like to continue our conversation and invited me to sit with him and his wife on a bus ride to a barbeque in his honor the next afternoon.

On the bus we had a more wide-ranging conversation about his work in Brazil, his books, and his work in the United States. He was so gracious and engaging that it was easy to overcome my awe-inspired inarticulateness. By the time we arrived at the picnic site, we had also gone through all but the last question on my list. I left the gathering before he did and did not have any opportunity to talk with him further until the last day of the conference.

On that final day, I had competing emotions. I wanted to ask Freire the last question on the graduate students' list, but was reluctant to seek him out to do so. That question was the most difficult because it was a question that arose from a deep discomfort some students had with the implications for his work on power, oppression, and power-lessness. It was a question I was unable to answer myself in spite of having read much of his work. While I was trying to figure out a way to ask the question should I get a chance, Freire and I literally ran into each other when he was exiting an elevator I was set to en-ter. He greeted me by name and asked if we had gotten through the questions. I hesitatingly said in fact that I had one more. He invited me to ask it. "Given your work," I said, "we want to know 'where is the hope?'"

With little hesitation he moved toward me, took my face in his hands, looked me in the eyes, and said, "You tell them, 'you are the hope, because the theory needs to be reinvented, not replicated . . . it is a guide. We make history as we move through it, and *that* is the hope.'" If I said anything in return, I can't remember because I was overcome by emotion. I do remember that as he left, I stood rooted to the floor unable to move because of the power of this encounter. Here was a volume of meaning and conviction no amount of reading of his work could have conveyed.

There is no end to this story, because all the details have stayed with me. This incident left me humbled and yet energized. Considering that I came to the experience with the full expectation of "receiving" his wisdom, his words and actions stood in direct contrast to his "banking concept." I was immediately more committed to my work, I now had a fuller understanding of his, and I had a gift to bring back to the graduate students. This is an incident that contributes to a wider and deeper vision of my teaching.

I have had other experiences of profound engagement and learning outside of formal classrooms: the impact of reading Toni Morrison's Nobel Lecture (1994), the flash of insight that came from a particularly vivid research experience in the stacks of the Library of Congress, and the autumn walk with my colleague (talked about in the Preface) that became the impetus for writing this book. There is a Greek word, *peripeteia*, that, though originally applying to literature, evolved to have a more general meaning that fits here: the definition is "an unexpected reversal of circumstances; a sudden or dramatic change" (*Oxford English Dictionary*). The "Bringing Questions to Freire" story has this element, as do some of the other stories I have recounted here and in Chapter One. It is likely that some of your stories also have an element of peripeteia.

Now I invite you to recall a set of additional incidents, this time from your professional biography:

Think back on your professional life. What are at least three stories generated from some aspect of your professorial work outside of teaching? They may be about a person (like the Freire story), or they may be about a book or a research experience or a conference experience, for instance. As before, write down a few identifying phrases to bring each incident into focus. After identifying this last group of stories, you will return to them all in Chapter Three and begin to identify which ones rise to the level of "critical incidents." What are at least three stories that come to mind when you think about the professional realm of your career?

There are now three groups of episodes in the collection offered within this chapter, incidents gleaned from three different contexts: others' classrooms, your own classrooms, and other professional venues. How can these episodes contribute to your reflections on teaching? The process is not unlike working to write your name backwards with your nondominant hand as was suggested in the earlier part of this chapter; the deliberateness of this task demands conscious attention. In a book of essays entitled *Staying Put: Making a Home in a Restless World* (1993), Scott Russell Sanders describes the challenging process of purposeful reflection: "We are all amateurs when it comes to knowing our place in the web of things . . . the work of belonging to a place is never finished" (p. xvi). Although his reference is to a physical space, I also perceive Sanders's reflection as a metaphor for the professional space in our lives. By combining the stories built into our syllabi, vita, and professional writing (each discussed in Chapter One), with the stories built in classrooms (discussed at the beginning of this chapter) and with the stories remembered with prompting, the storied landscape of our lives begins to become clear; the "web of things" begins to gain visibility.

Repertoire

Giving each recalled story a title will make it easier to identify the exceptionalities of the incidents. Look at the few words you used to describe each story and give each story a name. Pick a few keywords that are a type of shorthand for the scope of each story, maybe one of the brief identifying details you jotted down, and construct a personal "table of contents." In my own work, the table of contents looks like this (some of these stories I have already retold in this book, others I will tell later):

Stories where I have been a learner:

a.   Miss Hentges's Recognition (Chapter Two)

b. Grad School Decision (Chapter One)

c. Mr. Berg's Comment (Chapter Eight)

Stories where I have been a teacher:

a. Kirby's Paper (Preface)

b. Winter Saturday Classroom (Chapter One)

c. Students Asked Me to Leave (Chapter One)

d. Using Wait-time (Chapter Two)

e. Shoulder-Shrugger (Chapter Four)

f. Students Applaud Students (Chapter Three)

g. First Day (Chapter Six)

Stories from professional venues:

a. Walk with Sharon (Preface)

b. Library Firing (Chapter One)

c. Bringing Questions to Freire (Chapter Two)

d. Perception of Credibility (Chapter Eight)

Your table of contents needs to make sense only to you. Each title is meant to link memories to you so this list can serve as a reference point for the next steps. If one story has elements of more than a single category within it, I suggest you still list it in only one place. If you've recalled more than three incidents in any group, include those also. The goal is to approach the first stage of analysis in the next chapter with a rich repertoire of incidents.

Simply reviewing the list of titles can provide some overarching observations. The span of years the stories represent may be broad (mine run through more than fifty years) or narrow. Collectively, the stories may lean more toward interactions or to solitude. These

may be stories that overall have been repeatedly retold or only recently remembered. The details may be vivid or hazy. They may
be stories told to new acquaintances on airplanes, like the one I
recounted in Chapter One, or shared with friends. Or not shared
at all. For some reason these are stories that persist. At an early
point in Ibsen's play *Peer Gynt*, Aase says this about her young son
when she realizes the impact that myths and legends have had on
his perception of reality: "But who would have thought the . . . tales
would have clung to him so?" (1867/1992, p. 32). By moving from
a list of recollections to taking a closer look at the characteristics
of each, it becomes possible to pay attention to why some stories
"cling."

Next Steps

This chapter opened with a discussion of the ways "story-making"
and "story-telling" are different dimensions of Gudmundsdottir's
story-building that go on in classrooms as faculty teach a course.
Story-making, she says, involves the selection and organization of
the content. In some ways, the process of recalling nine or more
stories parallels this story-making stage: the list of titles organizes
the story-making from one's educational biography into a type of
outline. In subsequent chapters the elaboration and analysis will
delve into the story-telling phase (Gudmundsdottir describes this
dimension as adding personal and metaphorical details to the content). These two processes begin to enable the landscape of our
professional lives to come into sharper relief. Earlier in this chapter, Maxine Greene's words were used at the beginning of this process of gathering stories. Her words carry more meaning now at the
conclusion of these initial steps of gathering stories: "To be in touch
with our landscapes is to be . . . aware of the ways we encounter the
world" (1978, p. 2).

In Chapter One, the storied contexts of college teaching were
set out for reflection. In this chapter, a series of autobiographical

stories were identified, retold, and organized. The work in Chapter Two leads to Chapter Three, where a series of codings will be applied to identify a subset of "critical incidents." We will pursue responding to this question: How do stories from our personal and professional landscapes have lives beyond their mere telling?

3

Storied Accounts

*The point, I think, would be to speak of what has left
indelible impressions. But I discover such impressions
slowly, often long after the fact.*

(Glück, 1994, p. 4)

To illustrate the storied context of college teaching, Chapter One described how stories frame university work in unexpected ways. Chapter Two provided opportunities to identify a repertoire of incidents from our educational biographies that are memorable enough to be recalled years after they have occurred. In this chapter, those stories serve as the starting point for the next step of identification of critical incidents. These will become sites for analysis in later chapters. A description of a classroom event written by math professor Leonid Khazanov (2007) illustrates how a single incident left an indelible impression and led to his reflections on teaching.

Professor Khazanov describes walking into his Math 010 class and completely losing his voice midway through the class period. Although he considers dismissing the class, one of his students speaks up and offers, "I can teach this topic for you" (p. 162). This brief experience served as an impetus for self-reflection because Khazanov had to make an immediate decision, and he was not entirely comfortable turning the class over to a student. Khazanov writes about this moment as a "remarkable" and "significant development" in his understanding of his teaching (p. 161). "When the Instructor Must Take the Back Seat" is an essay in which he talks about this classroom story as a catalyst for reflection. His initiating story is not unlike one of mine—"Students Asked Me to Leave"—and you may have found it is similar to one of those that you might have recalled when responding to the three prompts in Chapter Two.

For Khazanov, the story is about more than an offer a student makes—it is about his reaction to what happened next: "[S]tudents rose to an unthinkable level in initiative and independence" (p. 157). His assumptions about student ability did not lead him to expect this to happen. Through reflection, he gains new insights into his teaching and illustrates that such reflection may start with looking out the windows of stories, but can lead to opening doors into one's teaching present (and presence). His essay is about more than sharing an entertaining anecdote. His reflection and the critical reflection this book pursues involve more: "This is not just a matter of writing down one's educational experiences . . . rather the benefit consists in critical reflection on those experiences to understand what principles and patterns have been at work in one's educational life" (Cortazzi, 1993, p. 13).

In this chapter an application of a series of codings for stories generated in Chapter Two will lead to an identification of those of your personal stories that reach the threshold of "critical incident." This process is one in which, as it is in Professor Khazanov's essay and in my story "Students Asked Me to Leave," an "autobiographical account of educational experience serves to mark the site for excavation" (Grumet, 1981, p. 122). A brief clarification of the term "critical incident" will be useful before proceeding with this "excavation."

Defining Terms

The terms *incident, event, story,* and *anecdote* are used here interchangeably to describe experiences similar to Professor Khazanov's classroom story. In "Storytelling as Inquiry," Reason and Hawkins state simply that, in their work, a "story" is "any event retold from life which appeared to carry some meaning, however small ..." (1988, pp. 89–90). There is a rich vein of literature that sets forth more complex distinctions among the terms listed above, but the words are being used here in the colloquial rather than in the technical sense. The phrases "critical incident" and its synonym, "critical event" (Webster and Mertova, 2007, p. 75), however, do need a brief discussion to provide background on their use. Critical incidents are the primary focus of the subsequent analysis and reflection as we pursue what we can learn through our stories.

When the word *critical* precedes the word *incident* or *event*, the two-word phrase has a specific meaning: "Critical events," Webster and Mertova write, "are 'critical' because of their impact and profound effect on whoever experiences such an effect ..." (p. 77). In an earlier work, Woods (1993) similarly addresses the use of the term *critical* and says that such incidents are "critical in the sense of [being] crucial, key, and momentous" (p. viii).

What makes a story a "critical incident"? Critical incidents differentiate themselves from other events by being "flashpoints" (Woods, 1993, p. 1), "jolting events" (Eakin, 2008, p. 3), and "highly charged moments and episodes that have enormous consequences for personal change and development" (Sikes, Measor, and Woods, 1985, p. 230). The use of the term "critical incident" in this book draws from previous work linking the identification of them to subsequent professional reflection. The usefulness of the approach has been established in the literature, but the adaptations here deepen its focus.

In the nearly sixty-year period since Flanagan (1954) introduced a "critical incident technique," there has been a series of major works in education that focus on critical incidents and critical events. *Critical Incidents in Teaching* is the title of each of the four works that follow (listed chronologically to illustrate the progression): Corsini and Howard (eds.), 1964; Killen and Mc-Kee, 1983; Tripp, 1993; and Woods, 1993. All four works address incidents in K–12 teaching. Other sources have titles that indicate a more specific application of the term "critical incident." Measor authored an essay (1985) in Ball and Goodson's edited book on critical incidents "in the classroom." Brookfield described it in "Using Critical Incidents to Explore Learners' Assumptions" (1990) and later, used a "critical incident questionnaire" to garner learners' perceptions of their learning experiences (2006). In pinpointing a more precise use, Webster and Mertova (2007) subtitled their book "Using Critical Event Narrative Analysis in Research on Learning and Teaching."

While the work undertaken here in the three stages of critical reflection on teaching draws on these previous sources, the context for the term "critical incident" differs from the briefly cited literature in three major ways:

1. The critical incidents are drawn from a broader range of events in an educational biography;

2. This book seeks to guide faculty in the process of their own internal search for assumptions and to link these to areas of professional growth in teaching; and

3. The critical incidents identified for reflective attention are seeded in the life histories of college teachers rather than in the classroom settings of elementary and secondary school teachers. (In the sources cited above, only Brookfield and Webster and Mertova address contexts other than K–12.)

Responding to the Incidents

It is in the context of college teaching that professors themselves define the concept of "critical incident" when they write about their own experiences. They consistently describe the strong emotional responses that incidents generate, and this is the next stage of our work on the stories identified in Chapter Two.

Reflections like Professor Khazanov's, which opened this chapter, illustrate what Jalongo and Isenberg mark as "the features that elevate a teacher's story from the realm of idle talk ... authenticity, reflection, and response" (1995, p. 12). When other college teachers chronicle their professional growth, their accounts also often begin with a description of their strong response to one particular event. The authors move to reflect on their response to an incident itself. Three examples from professors in different disciplines place the definition of "critical incident" into a practical rather than theoretical context and illustrate the significance of a heightened emotional response. These examples will help you see the nature of critical incidents. In the section following these professors' stories you will be introduced to the process for identifying them within your own list.

When management professor Fernanda Duarte (2007) agreed to join her colleagues in a curriculum redesign project, she unexpectedly found herself involved in much more than a perfunctory committee assignment. In retrospect, she found this professional development experience was a "catalyst for profound change in the self as teacher" (p. 9). She describes the experience as engendering "feelings of euphoria, enlightenment and excitement ... uncertainty, ambiguity and frustration" (p. 3). As part of an intercultural communications course, Professor Lori Carrell (2007) led undergraduates on a trip to the Amazon rainforest. She expresses "astonishment" at how students responded so profoundly when the learning conditions under which the students worked were the very conditions she had tried to *prevent* in her own campus classroom: "high anxiety, significant discomfort, frustration, anxiety, danger, and exhausting labor" (p. 1). She says a consequence of this for her was that she had to reexamine assumptions she held about learning; she "was driven to know what happened, and that's when the real adventure began" (p. 1). The text of an e-mail to Business Professor Thomas Hawk is what led him to think deeply about some assumptions that he held about student learning (Hawk and Lyons,

2008). "Please," the student e-mail began, "do not give up on me in this class" (p. 316). For Hawk and his colleague, Paul Lyons, this incident led to their probing of student responses to learning in order to scrutinize their own teaching practices. Collectively the events that led to these college teachers' reflections on their teaching distinguish themselves because they carry an "unusually high emotional charge" that has "a continuing significance" (Tripp, 1993, p. 98).

The telling of the stories can take many forms. In the multiple examples within this chapter, professors like Khazanov tell their stories to colleagues through their essay writing. Some professors, like Jane Tompkins (A Life in School, 1996), tell their stories in extended pieces of writing, while other professors join together to tell them in edited books like Wise Women: Reflections of Teachers at Midlife (Freeman and Schmidt, eds., 2002). The twenty-seven reflective narratives in the Freeman/Schmidt collection trace the roots of contributors' practices through the routes of their implications in their lives. Emerging as a part of the act of telling, sociology professor Esther Ngan-Ling Chow (in the Wise Women collection) finds, "Coalescence of the crosscurrents of my private and public lives has very much shaped the meanings and ways in which I have learned from teaching and have learned to teach" (p. 197). Consider the impact that the act of telling a story has on the teller.

Telling Stories

In my experience, each time I tell a story some new detail comes to light as I try to communicate the essence of the incident to someone else. It has been years, for instance, since I have told the story "Kirby's Paper." As I was writing the Preface for this book and telling it there, I recognized that the simple lesson I had originally drawn from the event ("labels aren't forever") applied as much to me as I grew in my teaching as it did to students like Kirby. Taking the time to tell one or more of your stories to someone else can serve not only for you to engage with a family member, friend, or colleague, but also to contribute to the "re-storying" of the incident itself. Recalling a story and jotting down a few details and a brief title in Chapter Two may have, in fact, made you *want* to tell the story to someone. In telling a story, whether orally or in writing, we make choices about which details to include and exclude, which events will be glossed over or elaborated, and what motivations and responses will be foregrounded or left unacknowledged: "The teller's own thought process is one of the potential sources of richness in storytelling: the teller may be telling one story about something that happened and a second story about the evolution of his or her understanding of events as they are being narrated" (Ferguson, n.d., p. 1).

Look over your list of titles and consider telling one or more of them to someone.

> If there is the opportunity to do so, tell one or more of your stories to someone. Listen to how your story evolves in response to the reactions, questions, and comments that invite you to elaborate the story as you tell it. Doing this can enrich your memories and thus make contributions to "the teller, the tale, and the told." (Killick and Frude, 2009, p. 850)

Introducing Descriptive Symbols

This chapter opened with lines from an essay written by poet Louise Glück. In these lines she wrote about how important it is to consider what has left "indelible impressions." The task here is to make that consideration a concrete one. It is one thing to retell a memorable event; it is another to articulate what specific response to the event led to its making that "indelible impression." Collectively the events that led to the college teachers' reflections included earlier in this chapter distinguish themselves because they carried an "unusually high emotional charge" that had "a continuing significance" (Tripp, 1993, p. 98). Rather than write out each of the stories listed at the conclusion of Chapter Two and then undertake a content analysis to look at "reflection and response" (Jalongo and Isenberg, 1995, p. 12), the approach here is simpler but still purposeful in seeking those stories that have the most emotional significance.

A series of symbols will be used to identify which of a range of responses you tie to each incident. When I look back at "Students Asked Me to Leave," I can pretty easily recount the details of what happened, but recalling the reasons such a story has stayed with me all these years involves a different layer of "telling." Applying a set of symbols, each representing a type of response, helps me reach *into* the story. Each symbol serves as a code, and with the application of the code to one or more incidents, some of your stories will end up having a few codes and others more. You have a list of the story titles from Chapter Two: what responses are among those that have contributed to the stories being the ones you recalled? The next step guides you in responding to this question.

Applying Symbols

In reflecting on "Bringing Questions to Freire," I know there are a tangle of reactions I had at the time and have had since. There is the overall impact of the story (I can barely tell the story without getting emotional), but there is also a host of feelings I had at different times throughout the incident. In order to look at the impact of this story alongside others (like "Miss Hentges's Recognition"), I have found that "naming" some of those reactions through applying some symbols to each story helps me understand which have had a more influential impact than others.

The list of response codes below is not a comprehensive one, but it does include a range of reactions that will likely apply in different ways to one or more of your stories. Each of the symbols is followed by a brief description. By now, you might have already begun to differentiate between entertaining anecdotes and incidents of stronger significance. Applying these codes will help you make this distinction and see how reactions lend powerful meanings to some vignettes we still carry with us.

Here is the list of symbols and a brief description of the reaction each relates to. Following this list are specific examples of their use and suggestions for how to proceed with the coding of your own stories.

Codings for Incidents

* This was something **unexpected**; it threw me off my usual course.

@ This was something **rewarding**; it was gratifying.

! This was something **unsettling**; it made me uncomfortable, even disoriented or anxious.

^ This was something **satisfying**; it gave me a sense of fulfillment.

% This was something **discordant**; it clashed with my previous experiences.

~ This was something **confirming**; it supported my previous experiences.

+ This made me **uncertain** or questioning; it made me unsure of my role or goal.

& This was something **contentious**; it made me angry or argumentative.

This was **exhilarating**; it energized me.

= This was **frustrating**; it confused me.

This book opened with the story about me playing school with my younger siblings ("Winter Saturday Classroom" in my list at the end of Chapter Two). The incident included some frustration (=) about my lack of firm control over my brother and sisters, but overall, I remember that I felt satisfied (^) by the experience. On the other hand, I have more of a range of responses as I recall "Students

Asked Me to Leave." In that incident, students asked me to leave the classroom and stay in my office for two class periods so that they could review the prerequisite skills for the course. At various times during this incident, I recall feeling disoriented (!), thrown off my usual course (*), uncertain (+), frustrated (=), that it clashed with my previous experience (%), and eventually rewarded (@).

My suggestion is that as you apply the codes to your own list of incidents you do so quickly, taking your first impression of the applicability of each symbol. As you do this you may feel that little distinguishes one code from another. You are the one interpreting both the codes and the stories, so even if one code seems to duplicate another continue to apply it down your list of stories because it may still bring some reactions to light. I find that approaching the coding quickly without stopping to analyze each application is the most useful way to help me see what contributed to their being an indelible part of my professional biography. Begin with your list of story titles, and the list of codes.

> Starting with the first symbol, look at your list of story titles and mark that symbol next to any of the stories to which the description following the symbol applies. Continue the process with each of the codes, taking the symbol through the list of story titles and placing it next to any of the incidents that it matches. What do you remember as your reaction at the time the incident occurred?

Because the steps in the reflective process in this book build on each other, it is important to have matched the codes with the stories to which they apply before proceeding. The brief amount of time this step takes enables you to identify critical incidents from within the list of stories you generated in Chapter Two.

Differentiating Critical Incidents

Applying the symbols to my own stories, I found some incidents have only two codes (like "Winter Saturday Classroom") and some incidents have six codes each ("Students Asked Me to Leave," "Shoulder-Shrugger," "First Day," "Perception of Credibility," and "Students Applaud Students"). The rest of my stories have a number of codes within that range. This suggests that as I remember the stories, some incidents carry more emotional weight than others. One of the signifiers of a "critical incidents" is this: they "are 'critical' because of their impact and profound effect on whoever experiences such an event" (Webster and Mertova, 2007, p. 77). The stories with the most symbols have a heightened level of effect that differentiates them from the others. Specifically, note those stories that fall together into the group with the most codes. Here is the collection of the critical incidents that will become your focus for analysis in subsequent chapters.

The emotional strength of some of your responses to a story *not* in your group of critical incidents may have a level of significance that matches or exceeds those you marked with more codes. Reviewing your list of stories and their accompanying codes will assist you in understanding what the process may not reveal. For instance, the "Bringing Questions to Freire" story I told in Chapter Two has five codes and is not in my top group. But, the power of the responses that story *does* generate for me matches the response power of those incidents in my most significant group. I would include it as one of my critical incidents because I am aware of how deeply it affected me even though the coding process did not reflect that.

Use the number of symbols next to each story as the initial guide for identifying what for you are critical incidents. Mark those stories that have the highest number of symbols. One-third of the stories in your repertoire is a rough estimate of how many are likely to emerge as critical incidents, but that is a general idea only. Then, consider stories that were not in this top group. Is there an additional story with fewer symbols where your response was such that you feel it matches the intensity the others? If so, consider adding it to your list of critical incidents. List this subset of story titles that have reached a threshold of being critical incidents.

After this coding step you may have gained some insight into powerful stories that have accompanied you along your professional way. Use those insights to delve deeper into the incidents in the next step. At different stages this will be a process of surprise—some surprises resonant and some likely discordant. Along that continuum will be opportunities to reflect on insights as you seek to understand the implications of the stories.

The analysis that begins in Chapter Four will be best served by your working with three to six critical events—more than that may be overwhelming as you undertake work in the next stages, and fewer will make the "assumption hunting" more difficult. Stories *not* identified as critical incidents will, however, still be a part of testing out the themes and assumptions that emerge, so they will play a role in the reflection undertaken here.

The work done up to this point in the chapter is intended to begin the process of looking more deeply into your critical incidents—in ways not unlike how the professors whose stories were cited wrote about insights they gained from incidents they responded to. This "burrowing" process (Connelly and Clandinin, 1990, p. 11) began with the few descriptive phrases jotted down early in Chapter Two and continues now with a brief elaboration of the responses the coding process prompted.

Elaborating Critical Incidents

As you have seen in your own application of the codes, not all of the stories we remember are identified in this process as being critical incidents. Were you to repeat the process a few years from now, you would probably find some other story that rises to that level (not necessarily a more recent one). I find that there are a finite number of stories that rise to that level for me, and the work of looking into those stories is not unlike how the grain of wood is revealed on the wheel of a skillful wood turner. Doing this work on critical reflection, I have come to understand "Students Applaud Students" as one of my few critical incidents, and it has not been shared yet in this book. I tell it here to illustrate what additional details the elaboration process contributes.

Students Applaud Students

My goal for this class period was to teach undergraduate education majors in the "Measurement and Evaluation" course the difference between norm-referenced and criterion-referenced testing. I had confidently prepared a lecture that included definitions, examples, and a graphic illustration. To me this was an easy pair of concepts to differentiate. I was eager to explain the terms to students and move on to its implications. When I finished my explanation, however, students' faces told me that my planning had been for naught. No hands went up when I asked simple recitation questions, and students looked puzzled, even confused. This was a surprise to me because both their reading and my well-prepared lecture covered the material thoroughly. I resorted to repeating my examples more slowly and deliberately. Still, no signs of understanding. Eventually, my own frustration with their inability to grasp the distinctions and my own inability to offer different examples or alternative explanations led me to mentally throw my hands in the air and direct them to a group task: "Get into small groups, use your class notes and text, and come up with a metaphor that clarifies these concepts." I did not know where this impromptu assignment came from. Today, I surmise that because it is a process I personally use when trying to understand something complex, it was a default mode for me. I know that I thought assigning them a task would buy me some time to rethink the lesson.

After I explained what a metaphor is and gave some examples, they set to work. Surprisingly, they worked diligently and appeared to be purposefully engaged. Because I was so struck by their level of involvement, I did not work on revising my own explanation. At the conclusion of the time allotment, each group took a few minutes to present their metaphor. Overall, the comparisons that they made were useful and clarifying. One group in particular announced they were going to present "the best" metaphor. I remember that they did—their explanation went right to the heart of the distinction between the concepts; they knew it and so did their class colleagues. Their classmates spontaneously erupted in applause. Because this response was so memorable for me, I regrettably have forgotten their metaphor. In this story I was stunned by many things, but the memory of their success and the applause stunned me the most.

When I identified which response symbols applied to this story during the coding process, the result was that I felt six of the descriptions resonated with my recollection. My response to this incident was that it was *unexpected* (∗), *unsettling* (!), *discordant* (%), *frustrating* (=), in some moments, *contentious* (&), and it made me feel *uncertain* (+). In your reading of this account, you may see other codings, but as the "teller of the tale" I apply those codings based on my own reflection. With this coding I realized that this is one of my critical incidents.

The goal of the next phase of the process in this chapter is to elaborate your responses to each critical incident and to identify the reasons behind the symbols that you paired with those particular stories. The details uncovered in this elaboration phase will provide further insights that will contribute to your taking a closer look at themes within and across the stories. Adding a "because" statement after each symbol paired with a story will prompt you to articulate some of the reasons why you remembered those particular stories. Here is the elaboration of the codes for the "Students Applaud Students" critical incident in my repertoire.

For the story "Students Applaud Students" I felt the events were

* unexpected – *because* students successfully taught themselves

! unsettling – *because* they taught more effectively than I did

% discordant – *because* I had previously had little success with group work

+ uncertain – *because* I had no back-up plan for teaching the material

+ frustrating – *because* I was convinced I was prepared

& contentious – *because* my view was that they had not prepared for class

As I write these *because* statements, it becomes clearer to me both then and now that there are many elements of the story that surprised me. Novelist Isabel Allende's words in her novel *Eva Luna* (1989) metaphorically describe what happens as story details emerge. She explains a particular place as "having as many layers as phyllo dough" (p. 211). Naming a story, telling it to someone, and then exploring its personal impact guides us into some of the layers of memory.

The process for this next elaboration step, a step meant for you to begin to explain just such layers, is similar to that for the coding step: by moving quickly, taking the first thing that comes to mind, more details of the story will begin to emerge.

Begin with the title of one of the critical incidents you have identified in your repertoire and the codes listed with it. For each code add a brief "because" statement. Work quickly, but if something does not come to mind immediately, leave it and then come back to it when the other codes have been elaborated. If some of the "because" statements seem repetitious, see if you can be even more specific in your reflection so you can capture some of the finer details. Why was that response at the forefront of your mind when you were engaged in the coding process? Go through this process with each of your critical incidents.

The concept of peripeteia (an unexpected reversal of circumstances), discussed in Chapter Two, describes a characteristic of memorable incidents. It may have more meaning now after the use of the coding and elaboration process. Jerome Bruner discusses the term and follows it up by explaining, ". . . the impetus to narration is expectation gone awry" (2002, p. 2). The next elaboration step is likely to make the "expectations gone awry" more visible.

The phrase "gone awry" may sound like it refers to a negative disruption, but it may also be one with more positive overtones. In my "Bringing Questions to Freire" story, the expectation that I carried to the conference was that someone of Freire's prominence would be inaccessible. My expectation went awry when he actually invited me to engage in an ongoing conversation—a conversation that took place over a few days because of his warmth, grace, and openness; the result was a positive disruption of my stereotype-based expectation. This is in contrast with the "Students Applaud Students" story where I carried a different set of expectations. My major expectation was that I held the keys to students learning the content and that group work would be a sharing of their ignorance. When a series of events happened in class to counter that, my expectations went awry.

Now that you have identified a small number of critical incidents and briefly elaborated them with "because" statements, there is one additional elaboration that will be useful. By quickly identifying a major expectation that undergirds each of your critical incidents, more of the "texture" or dimensions of the stories will begin to come into focus.

Briefly consider one major expectation that was at the heart of each of your critical incidents and was challenged in the course of the story.

This prompt may assist you: "A major expectation I held at the beginning of this story was . . ." After you have concluded this step, each of
the critical incidents will have a title, a set of codes, a set of "because"
statements, and now an expectation statement.

A Note on Process

To reiterate a point made in the Preface, there are multiple ways
to engage with this reflective process. The book is written to guide
you in independently reflecting on your own work. However, the
experience could be enhanced by going through the process with a
colleague or a small group of colleagues where the notes and writing
are augmented through telling the stories to each other. The process
of this book focuses on reflecting on stories, but in fact, stories are
meant to be told.

If you have gotten this far into the book without having explored your stories using the suggested process, I encourage you to
delve into the details of your stories in a parallel way that works
for you. There is flexibility in this heuristic process; the steps are
intended as an overall strategy with prompts to guide gathering
and elaborating on memorable stories. The very word *heuristic*, derived from the Greek meaning "to guide in discovery or investi-
gation," contrasts with approaching the process of narrative inquiry through an algorithmic one (Jalongo and Isenberg, 1995, pp.
175–176, drawn from work in Rosenshine and Meister, 1992, p.
26). The heuristic process in this book is less a lock-step, objective
procedure and more a flexible, recursive one.

The process that frames the data-gathering steps is guided by
four overarching questions. They can similarly be used if you are
seeking additional flexibility in the suggested process: (1) Which
stories from your educational biography are easily remembered?
(2) What happened in each? (3) What responses do you remember having for each at the time? (4) For key—critical—incidents,
what was a primary expectation you held that needed to be

reevaluated at that time? Each set of prompts provided for some flexibility ranging from the number of stories identified, how the codes were applied during the coding process, how many details were included in a brief sketch, and which and how many critical incidents were pinpointed for further analysis.

The following outline uses these framing questions to review the process identified in each segment within the last two chapters. This outline may be useful to augment work you have already done or to modify the steps that will enable you to complete the material that will be used beginning in Chapter Four.

Which stories from your educational biography are easily remembered? Three prompts were used to provide structured guidance for recalling at least nine stories from various contexts.

1. *What happened in each story at the time?* The invitation was to write down a few memory-jogging details and to provide a brief descriptive title for each story.

2. *What responses do you remember having at the time of each incident?* A series of descriptive codes were applied to each story, and a subset of critical incidents were identified based on the strength of your emotional responses to them.

3. *For key, critical, incidents what was a primary expectation you held that needed to be reevaluated at the time because of the incident?* The articulation of one underlying expectation for each critical incident was invited.

Next Steps

This chapter opened with a discussion of the ways that professors have used critical incidents from their educational biographies as the impetus for professional reflection on their classroom practices. The impact of the stories that left "indelible impressions" (Glück, 1994, p. 4) on them led to their awareness of assumptions,

assumptions that these professors came to use in taking new looks at their teaching practices. A heuristic process framed by four overarching questions served to guide you in distinguishing critical events among the stories you generated at the conclusion of Chapter Two. The process here in Chapter Three had you elaborate on your critical incidents first in brief notes and then in the "telling of the tale" to someone else. The exploration undertaken in Chapter Three built on the identification of stories in Chapter Two; the initial analysis that will begin in Chapter Four will build on the attention paid specifically to the critical incidents identified in this chapter. Essayist Wendell Berry (1990) says that to "pay attention" has special imperatives:

> To pay attention is to come into the presence of a subject. In one of its root senses, it is to 'stretch toward' a subject, in a kind of aspiration. We speak of 'paying attention' because of a correct perception that attention is *owed*—that without our attention and our attending, our subjects, including ourselves, are endangered. (p. 83)

One way to "pay attention" is to scrutinize the stories in unexpected ways. This will begin in Chapter Four where themes in three areas will be considered: the role of the learner, the role of the teacher, and the role of the content. Polkinghorne (1988), whose influential review of the work on the use of narrative in the human sciences, observes, "The goal of analysis [of a collection of stories] is to uncover common themes . . ." (p. 177). And, as these common themes are uncovered in the upcoming chapters, the metaphorical "layers of phyllo dough" (Allende, 1989, p. 211) will begin to separate.

4

Seeking Patterns

Lives and their experiences are represented in stories.
They are like pictures that have been painted over,
and, when the paint is scraped off, something new
becomes visible.

(Denzin, 1989, p. 81)

The goal in Chapter Two was to open up a space for recalling stories and then in Chapter Three for retelling them. With the collection of stories and elaboration of a subset of critical incidents, the groundwork has been laid to begin looking at what can "become visible," as Denzin says in the opening quote. In the two-step process of analysis in this chapter, "when paint is scraped off," some initial patterns will begin to emerge.

Delving into critical incidents is grounded in approaching them as *Acts of Meaning* (in the words of a title of a 1990 book by Jerome Bruner). There are, Bruner writes, four interdependent "selves" present within the retelling of a story (p. 121). Becoming aware of this tangle of selves makes it possible to see where we, as storytellers, are situated in the process of analysis. There is, he describes, "the self then, the self now recalling then, the self now interpreting the self then from the present self's perspective, the self thinking about future selves" (p. 121).

The "self then" is who we were in the moment of the incident. Unless there was a video or audio recording or careful diary or journal entries, the precise details of the incident have been replaced by visual and emotional impressions vivid enough to bring the incident to life even years afterwards. The recollections that emerge when the "self now" tells the story of the "self then" have been shaped over the intervening years by additional experiences, stories, and insights. Chapters Two and Three invited this "self now" to retell incidents about the "self then." Most of this chapter continues that work in order to gather as many details as possible for subsequent interpretation.

The last section of this chapter provides initial steps for "the self now" *interpreting* the impact of the stories from the "self then." This precedes looking critically at the "self thinking about future selves" in the concluding chapter. While the contexts of Bruner's multiple selves that are present in the interpretation of stories is confusing, they illustrate an interrelatedness key to understanding the architecture of our storytelling. Each of Bruner's four selves contributes another layer of echoes that reverberate through our teaching lives. When the "self now" narrates the story of the "self then" there are multiple perspectives from which to choose to tell the story.

Considering Vantage Points

Stories about teaching-learning encounters can come in unexpected places. I was surprised when my first visit to a physician for a consultation on a knee injury turned into a lesson in storytelling. I began the office visit with a rapid-fire explanation of the accident that precipitated the appointment. Doc Losee interrupted me almost immediately and asked, "Who are you? Tell me that story first." I was speechless and switched gears to talk about why we had recently moved to rural Montana. Only after the storytelling did the talk shift to my injury. We became friends, extended family, actually, and he opens each conversation that we have with the same request: "Tell me the story about a recent day in your life." In this, he has been my teacher. College faculty tell stories through the teaching of classes, the construction of syllabi, and the writing about research—all illustrated in Chapter One—although rarely do friends or family approach us and directly request, "Tell me a story about your work." I was fortunate to meet Doc in the early 1970s; he taught me what it is like when another adult invites personal storytelling.

My "Doc Story" is, like others in my repertoire, a teaching-learning encounter where, in fact, there are multiple perspectives. I went into his exam room as a patient, but also as a student with the expectation that I would be taught how to alleviate pain. I wanted this physician to be an expert, to draw on his extensive knowledge and tell me what to do. My role, as I saw it, was to listen and follow his instructions. Doc tells the story differently (Losee, 1994, p. 164), and I could tell it differently, too. I might choose to tell it through the lens of the debilitating pain, or through the lens of the motorcycle accident. But I choose to tell it through my eyes as a student, with expectations of Doc as a teacher prepared to solve my problem. There are many stories here, each originating from a particular point of view—a vantage point.

Locating a vantage point within a story is not unlike looking at a basketful of multicolored yarns that have become a heap of intermingled strands. In an effort to separate the strands in preparation for a knitting project, the first step is to identify one colored strand with which to begin the untangling. A vantage point is similar because it is a place to begin the process of unraveling threads of a narrative. The starting place of the telling of a story contains a clue to identifying the initial vantage point: "I was a student in Miss Hentges's' class"; "I was the teacher in 'Measurement and Evaluation'"; "I approached Paulo Freire as a student approaches a highly respected teacher." In these instances, how I begin to recount each story makes my vantage point clear. In the first I am a student, in the second I am the teacher, and in the third, once again, I tell the story through my eyes as a student. These are, as poet Adrienne Rich describes, "small distinctions" but consequential ones:

> I promised to show you a map you say but this is a mural
> then yes let it be these are small distinctions where do
> we see it from is the question
>
> (Rich, 1991, p. 6)

The now-familiar details of the story may, through this stage, become unfamiliar, and "where you see it from" may illuminate new currents underneath the surface of the telling.

Determining Initial Vantage Points

By naming an initial vantage point in each of your three to six critical incidents, patterns can become more accessible. As you recall how you initially encountered each critical event, through which lens do you now enter the story? Do you tell the story through the eyes of a student or a teacher? How do you position yourself when you think about or tell each critical incident in relationship to other people in the story?

The story "Students Applaud Students" was used in Chapter Three to illustrate each of the steps so far in the process that leads to reflection on what our stories teach us. It can also serve in this chapter as an example of how each stage of pattern-seeking applies to a critical incident. To recap this incident, the story involved my unsuccessful attempt to explain two concepts (norm- and criterion-reference testing) to college juniors. I expected them to follow my explanation and examples and use them as tools to learn the material. They did not. When I gave a spur-of-the-moment small group assignment they were surprisingly able to teach themselves the concepts, and they ultimately broke into spontaneous applause over their success.

The vantage point or lens through which I recall and retell this event is as a teacher (my "self now recalling then"). It is the lens through which I recount my relationship with the students, the content, and the story's context. The "teacher then," as I now recount for myself, had a series of expectations that "went awry."

I determined the vantage point in "Students Applaud Students" through three signifiers: first, the role I use when I begin to tell the story; second, the lens through which I view and recount the relationships present in the story; and third, the perspective from which the expectations were held and the perspective from which I judged that those expectations where disrupted. My vantage point in this story is "teacher." With this recognition, I am better able to scrutinize the elements within the story as they are illuminated by that perspective.

For each critical incident, determine the vantage point (point of view) from which you retell the story either to yourself or someone else. Completing this prompt may help: "As I recall this critical incident I find myself thinking about it or telling it through the eyes of . . ." (for example, a student, a teacher, an observer). Although there are multiple points of view through which the story *could* be told, which vantage point do you adopt when you retell it?

Each critical incident now has notes on the following: a list of codes, an elaboration of each code with a "because" statement, one or more expectations that were confirmed or countered within the story, and with the above step, a vantage point that orients the telling. Throughout these chapters, a series of prompts are being suggested as a method to assist you in engaging deeply with the stories from your educational biographies. There are a number of methods that can be used to identify, elaborate, and note this information. Wilson's (2008) distinction between strategy and methods underscores that there are a number of ways to employ the strategy. "Methods are the means of transportation" (p. 39), and further, "it becomes possible to change methods as best suits the situation" (p. 39). *How* one accounts for, and delves into, the corners of the stories is more significant than a narrow compliance with a guiding prompt. This is choreography with inter-related steps. No matter how the notes on your critical incidents are recorded—on one sheet per incident, in a matrix, in a narrative, or in another format that meets your needs to jot reference notes for each incident—those constitute data that lead to the next stage in this chapter.

Describing Four "Commonplaces"

Articulating a vantage point can open new avenues for considering each incident. In the same way, looking through that lens to purposefully view the roles of the story elements embedded within each story can bring new points into focus. Because you have identified the critical incidents from a collection of stories in your educational biography, at the heart of each is a "teaching-learning encounter" (Schwab, 1973, p. 508). Such an event, as explained by Schwab, has four elements, or "commonplaces": learner, teacher, content, and context (p. 508). He posited that each of these four commonplaces makes a substantial contribution to how educational processes (both curriculum and instruction) should be studied, planned, and assessed.

Consider the story with which I opened the book, "Winter Saturday Classroom." It illustrates the ways that all four commonplaces are embedded in the telling of a teaching-learning encounter and the ways that the vantage point colors in the shape of each. I happily played the role of teacher, and that role was one of power assumed and power used. My brother and sisters were in the roles of learners, and their role in my retelling was primarily one of obedience. The content—or lessons—played a central role in how my relationship with my "pupils" evolved. And the contextual background had many components that figured into the story: I played a babysitting or care-taking function, I am the eldest, I was a good student myself, and the models of "teacher" in the popular culture of the fifties reinforced the role expectations I brought to this teaching-learning encounter. The role of this context was not as visible as those of the other commonplaces, but it was an influential one.

Because each of the critical incidents from your educational biography are in some form or other teaching-learning encounters, these four commonplaces serve as entry points to layers of meaning. Using the vantage point as a telescope magnifies the details of the story and brings the roles into sharper relief so they can be seen in new ways. Focusing attention on these singular elements will provide an opportunity to see roles, themes, and relationships among and between these stories, which forms a "hidden curriculum" in our professional development (Jalongo and Isenberg, 1995, p. 36). Different vantage points color the way the role of a teacher is conceptualized at the time of the story being told as the "self now" tells the story of the "self then." This will lead to an exploration of assertions underlying those patterns (Chapter Five), an articulation of three levels of assumptions (Chapters Six and Seven), and the implications of those assumptions for teaching practices and potential avenues for professional growth (Chapter Eight).

The Role of the Teacher within Each Critical Incident

Working with the ways that each critical incident positions the four commonplaces—teacher, learner, content, context—you are provided with the necessary keys for identifying assumptions that can enable insights into teaching practices. The "pathway to the present choice[s]" can be reconstructed "by digging under the layers of one's biography to identify encounters that led to it" (Grumet, 1976, p. 46). Whether the metaphor is Grumet's "digging under the layers" or Denzin's scraping the paint off a picture (1989, p. 81), the point is that teachers have a history. The extent of this history is not easily discernible, but scrutinizing the roles of the commonplaces, beginning with the role of the teacher, contributes to making it more apparent. The following brief examples illustrate this intersection between the vantage point through which the incident is told and the role of the teacher as seen from that perspective.

Illustration #1: In "Students Applaud Students," my initial vantage point as a teacher gives me a platform from which to describe the roles that each of the commonplaces plays in the incident. From this vantage point, I saw my teacher role as quite an inflexible one. At the time, I saw myself as an authoritarian information-giver, as a responsible intellectual, as a translator of the complex, as the disciplined leader with the responsibility to tell students what and how to learn.

Illustration #2: In the "Bringing Questions to Freire" incident, through my initial vantage point as the learner, I saw the teacher role (Freire's) as an authority, an expert, and an intellectual. My expectation of him in his role as teacher was that he would be awe-inspiring, inaccessible, and unapproachable, even though I hoped otherwise. There is an unexpected resonance here with the first critical incident. The role of "teacher" in both these stories has common elements.

Illustration #3: Here is another example from a chemistry professor who opens his essay "Lessons from Room 10" by reflecting on a formative experience from his own educational biography. In a recent issue of *The Teaching Professor*, he begins his reflection on teaching from the vantage point of a student, years earlier, in an advanced placement class that he took in chemistry: "I dreaded having to walk in there" (Cox, 2011, p. 6). From this vantage point, he describes the teacher as "mean," someone who "didn't create a supportive atmosphere," and someone who "gave her students an academic punch in the arm and it hurt" (p. 6).

In each of these incidents, looking at the role of the teacher from the vantage point of the teller enables an important glimpse of a formative image.

Select one of your critical incidents identified and elaborated on in Chapter Three. Use the primary vantage point from which you retell that particular story: How do you represent the role of "teacher" at the beginning of the incident? This prompt may assist: "From my perspective as I retell this story, I tell about the teacher as someone who ..."

If you were unable to narrow down the number of critical incidents through the coding and elaboration stages in the last chapter, use the critical incidents that you do have, and select three to six in which to characterize the role of the teacher. As you repeat this step for *each* of the critical incidents which you select, jot down a few notes for reference so that those notes can be used later in identifying patterns across the stories later in this chapter.

Work within *each* of your critical incidents from the vantage point through which you retell each story and describe the role of the teacher in the same way you just did for your first story: "From my perspective as I retell this story, I tell about the teacher as someone who ..."

The Role of the Learner within Each Critical Incident

Schwab says the second of the commonplaces that are a part of teaching-learning encounters is the learner. Whether we position ourselves in the story as the teacher, the learner, or the observer, the student role can be characterized from any of those vantage points. How we, as tellers, view our relationships with learners provides another avenue for gaining insights from our educational biographies. In this section of the chapter, an articulation of the role of the learner within each critical incident will augment the notes you have on the role of the teacher.

The following examples illustrate the role that the learner plays when using the same stories (and their vantage points) as before.

Illustration #1: In "Students Applaud Students," I recount the story from the vantage point of the teacher. From that perspective, I held an initial view of the role of learners that centered around my expectation of their respectful compliance. I held that their role in the initial stages of the story was to listen, absorb, respond, and learn. My role as teacher was inseparable from this expectation of their student role. Later, when through their actions they challenged my expectation, I experienced no epiphany. Their actions did, however, contribute a chink in the armor of my assumptions.

Illustration #2: I retell the "Bringing Questions to Freire" story through the vantage point of the student rather than the teacher. From that perspective, I saw my role as being respectful of the intellectual distance between us, reticent to approach someone of his authority, and aware of the importance of knowing my place in that setting. From my perspective here as the student, my perceived role kept me quieter than I wanted to be. When through our conversations my expectations were countered, I looked at this incident as an exception to the stereotypes that I held of our two roles.

Illustration #3: The chemistry professor's essay "Lessons from Room 10" (Cox, 2011) was told first from his view as the learner—a learner who saw his role as hesitant: "I hesitated before signing up for the class" (p. 6), curious: "something drew me to the experience" (p. 6), and willing to face challenges: "...we knew if we could survive 'Hell's Classroom,' we could take anything thrown at us in college" (p. 6).

Identifying the role of the learner in each of your three to six critical incidents makes an important contribution to "excavating" those incidents on the way to exploring their significance (Grumet, 1981, p. 122).

Work with your critical incidents identified and elaborated in Chapter Three. Use the primary vantage point from which you retell each story and jot down a few notes about how you viewed the role of the student at the beginning of the incident. It will be useful to do this with one or more of the incidents for which you described the role of the teacher in the previous step. This prompt may assist you: "From my perspective as I retell this story, I tell about the learner as someone who . . ."

When critical incidents were identified in Chapter Three, they were done so through a process of looking at the scope of responses each generated. The stories with the most extensive impact are likely to be the ones that provide the most deeply influential insights. Besides looking at the roles of the teacher and learner to move toward framing these insights, there are two additional elements that deserve attention, the role of content (which will be explored next) and the role of context (which will be explored in a later chapter on the roots of theory-building).

The Role of the Content within Each Critical Incident

The third of Schwab's commonplaces that are elements in teaching-learning encounters is the content. As the storyteller centers the story from a particular vantage point, the role of content emerges as a relational one. Interwoven between the teacher and learner, the content might appear in the foreground, it might be in the background, or it might not be immediately evident. It might even be irrelevant (also a role). The perspective from which the story is told is key because the central question is, "How did you, from your vantage point as the teller, see the presence of the content around which the teaching-learning encounter took place?"

Illustration #1: Even as I retell the "Students Applaud Students" story about the class in measurement and evaluation, the content of the lesson on norm- and criterion-referenced testing is the linchpin in this critical incident. The role of content from my vantage point as the teacher was primary. The role of content, in fact, trumped the role of learners. The content was something I felt was my responsibility to be proficient in. Both of these aspects had an impact on how I describe the role of the teacher and learner when I retell the story. Teasing out the role that content plays in each of my critical incidents begins to help me think more deeply about the legacy of each incident. In "Students Applaud Students," content was foregrounded.

Illustration #2: When I retell the "Bringing Questions to Freire" story and consider what role the content played, I relate it as the impetus for the conversation. The graduate students provided me with questions (the content) that as "student," I planned to glean from Freire's speeches and possibly from any questions I could ask him directly. My role as learner and his as teacher were both intertwined with this content. No content, no critical incident. But, when I look closely at what makes this memorable for me, the content recedes behind this teacher's commitment to engaging with that content. Here, content was in the background.

Illustration #3: The third story I have used as an example in this section of Chapter Four, chemistry professor James Cox's story, is one in which content plays a primary role. Content is, as he tells the story from his initial perspective as the student, daunting, challenging, and difficult. It is his major focus. Later in the essay and from his current perspective as a chemistry teacher himself, it is his relationship to the content he teaches in the class that reflects how he was influenced by the story. When descriptions of the role of the content in your critical incidents are added to notes being taken for each story, the impact of each incident gains additional dimensions.

Choose to look at more closely critical incidents in which you have described the roles of teacher and learner. Use the primary vantage point from which you recall each story. Jot down a few notes—in whatever form is meaningful to you—to describe the role that content plays in each story. This prompt may assist: "From my perspective as I retell this story, I tell about the content as something that . . ."

A Note on the Process

It is difficult work to take a handful of critical incidents that have been previously elaborated and then move deeper into the stories to characterize the role of the story elements in each. This process leads to looking at underlying currents that might otherwise be seen as anecdotes: it is, Pinar writes, "the autobiography that makes the self's architecture more complex, moves below the surface of memory" (1988, p. 28).

The process for getting to an awareness and examination of this "complex architecture" of one's teaching self cannot productively be presented in an oversimplified workbook. Contradictions, exceptions, and flexibility are a part of the stages because between those stages are semipermeable boundaries. The consequence, no matter what method you find works for you at each stage, can open you up to previously undiscovered insights. In a book that explores ways to reach deeper into our work, *Research Is Ceremony: Indigenous Research Methods*, the author says, "When ceremonies take place, everyone who is participating needs to be ready to step beyond the everyday and to accept a raised state of consciousness" (Wilson, 2008, p. 69). Seeking new avenues that lead to a deeper understanding of one's teaching self holds some of the elements about which Wilson writes. One of the challenges it is important to acknowledge within the process is its messiness: "Narrative language is unwieldy—like life—in refusing the artificial boundaries between reason and emotion, analysis and intuition, objectivity and subjectivity, process and product. These seeming opposites meld in stories ... making narrative analysis messy and challenging" (Wood, 2000, p. 445).

The goal of this stage is to locate some themes that repeat themselves in stories from earlier times to see what images live there. The richness—and messiness—of this work leads to understanding some of the unacknowledged currents flowing beneath the constant choice-making that is an inherent part of our teaching. The most memorable teaching-learning encounters in our lives have both obvious and subtle impacts—they are generally events that have helped us form our views and actions.

Pause. Sit with what you have discovered with these role statements. Like before, you may be surprised by new insights that doing this work has brought to the surface. The process of moving deeper into the stories will do more than simply fill in details; the visibility of some undercurrents of our views on teaching can come suddenly or evolve more slowly. The suggested process provides a framework for discovering stories that are old friends, whether or not you are just discovering them now or like me, you are revisiting stories you have told through the years. The critical incidents themselves create new stories as they are examined through a series of different lenses. One of those new stories will come to the fore by next looking at themes across the critical incidents.

Considering Role Patterns *across* Stories

Embedded across the critical incidents you are working with are four story lines, the story lines of the perceived roles of the teacher, learner, content, and context. (The fourth of Schwab's commonplaces, context, will be explored in a later chapter, as it relates to theory building.) Looking across critical incidents and briefly characterizing these three story lines adds additional information from which to explore propositions that we bring to teaching, propositions that contribute to our theory-in-use (Schön, 1983). The next step is to place the notes from the critical incidents side-by-side to consider what patterns emerge from the descriptions of the three commonplaces across the stories. The common elements that emerge will be unique because of personal contexts and the meaningful stories to which those personal contexts give rise. So, the process of the final step in this chapter echoes the action named in a title of a book of poetry by Demetria Martínez, *Breathing*

Between the Lines (1997). In this way, "interpretation is a revelatory enterprise" (Grumet, 1981, p. 128).

Among the three critical incidents of mine that I have drawn from for illustrations are "Students Asked Me to Leave" (included in Chapter One), "Students Applaud Students," and "Bringing Questions to Freire" (these last two included in Chapter Three). What follows is a glimpse of what I learned by undertaking this *cross-story* stage of reflection for the first commonplace, the role of the teacher. With my notes on the role of the teacher in each story placed side-by-side, I will read the characterizations as a group and then describe the common elements I see there.

Role of Teacher

Within each of my three critical incidents I see these roles:

"Students Asked Me to Leave"—from my vantage point as the teacher, my initial perception was that the role of the teacher was someone who was an expert, a director of learning, and an authority.

"Bringing Questions to Freire"—from my vantage point as the learner, my initial perception was that the role of the teacher was someone who was an expert, someone distant and unapproachable.

"Students Applaud Students"—from my vantage point as the teacher, my initial perception was that the role of the teacher was someone in charge, an expert and responsible director of learning.

Across each of my three critical incidents I see this role pattern:

No matter from which vantage point I retell the stories, I see that I initially perceived the role of teacher as the expert who directs learning from a place of power and authority. My retelling of these stories, no matter what the vantage point, converges in this role pattern.

My discovery of this role pattern was unsettling and is actually a rediscovery that I make writing this book. The repetition of themes is disconcerting because whenever I immerse myself in this process and analysis, I confront my own vulnerability. I feel as though a mirror has been placed in front of my face, and I am disoriented by what the reflection reveals. In *The Hitchhiker's Guide to the Galaxy*, author Douglas Adams vividly describes a reaction that is similar to mine at this stage of the analysis:

> When you're cruising down the road in the fast lane ... and are feeling pretty pleased with yourself and then accidentally change down from fourth to first instead of third thus making your engine leap out of your hood in a rather ugly mess, it tends to throw you off your stride ... (1979, p. 105)

I move to interpret the stories as I look across their themes (my "self now interpreting my self then") in order to gain insights into the underlying tensions that trip me up in my teaching, even today. I am willing to accept being disoriented because I know that there are insights to be gained about avenues for growth that impact students' success. In order to avoid being frozen in place by disconcerting surprises, it is useful at this stage to suspend judgment of any themes that come to the surface. Our biographies are not necessarily "prisons we live inside" (a variation on a title of Doris Lessing's book of essays, *Prisons We Choose to Live Inside*, 1994), but can be "prisms" through which we gain new perspectives, new hues, for our current thinking.

Approach this stage in whatever way enables you to explore and articulate patterns across stories. Reread what you described as the role of the teacher *within* each critical incident in order to identify any common elements that emerge *across* all of them. Briefly characterize what you find. What is the core perspective that you initially held about the role of the teacher, as revealed across three or four of your critical incidents?

> What is the core perspective you initially held about the role of the learner as revealed across these stories?
>
> What is the core perspective you initially held about the role of the content as revealed across these stories?

Once you have briefly described the patterns across critical incidents, a cross-check will be useful with a story that did *not* emerge as a critical incident. One of the incidents, for instance, that I listed as a part of my initial collection of stories in Chapter Two—"Shoulder-Shrugger"—can serve that role. It did not initially reach the level of critical incident in the coding stage of Chapter Three so this incident is a good choice for this double-checking.

Shoulder-Shrugger

About thirty years ago, I was teaching a class of sixty students, large enough that I knew students' faces before I knew their names. One particular student drew my attention from the first day because he seemed to respond negatively to most of what I said. He was a shoulder-shrugger. His nonverbal reactions to what I said in class escalated throughout the first month, and I grew increasingly agitated myself. The barely noticeable shoulder-shrug became an exaggerated shrug that was eventually accompanied by eye-rolling, head-tossing, and a wry smile at different points throughout each class. The more he exhibited this behavior, the more I narrowed my class planning to focus on teaching. I resolutely prepared each class with the goal of eliminating his reaction. I do not know if I grew more angry with him for his daily judgment of my teaching or with myself for my inability to stop it.

Even though a colleague whom I told about the shoulder-shrugger urged me to confront him directly, I struggled with exactly how to do that. At mid-term, he came to my office for one of the required visits. This was not an encounter I was looking forward to. When he entered the office he immediately announced he had something to say. Then, he pointed his finger at me in what appeared to me to be a threatening manner and said, "Whenever you tie theory to practice, I wonder *why* haven't any of my other professors done that before?" As he said this, he shrugged his shoulders, rolled his eyes, and shook his head from side to side. My expectations of a confrontation were unfounded. My certainty about my view of his motivation and my resolve to exert my power as his teacher were both unexpectedly countered. I was speechless and embarrassed. My presumption had totally colored the way I saw him and myself, and it had the effect of obscuring the other students in class from my view. We did then talk about class and his work. During the remainder of the course he spoke with me frequently, and I returned to broadening the focus of my teaching to encompass the entire class.

The summary role statements that resulted from my scrutinizing critical incidents upon reflection do resonate with this story: from my point of view as teacher ("I was a teacher in . . ."), my role was to be in control of content and to be responsible for (and the judge of) student reactions; my perception of the role of this student was that he should not challenge my competence or authority; my perception of the role of the content, in combination with my expertise, was as a controlling feature of the class.

The themes in this incident do align with the major characteristics of the themes embedded across my critical incidents. Again, the picture that is emerging of some underlying expectations of the teacher, learner, and content are disconcerting. I find this to be difficult to articulate because it touches on what I think about as the *history* of my growth as a teacher, but not in any way related to who I am in classrooms today. When I undertook the progressive process described in this book, however, I have come to recognize that some of the themes are in fact an influence on how I make current pedagogical decisions. Reflecting on what I am learning here, however, is like standing between two mirrors where they are positioned to make an unending series of diminishing images blurry, but obliquely recognizable. With the next steps in upcoming chapters, further work on the "self now interpreting the self then" will lead to the "self thinking about future selves."

Next Steps

The initial chapter in this book illustrated how we tell stories in our professional lives through multiple activities related to teaching, learning, and scholarship. Then, in Chapter Two, through remembering stories *about* teaching and learning, and in Chapter Three, considering why some of the stories get repeatedly retold, the stories began to contribute to a portrait of our educational biographies.

This chapter opened with an example of the ways that the vantage point through which stories are told contributes to shaping which details receive attention in the retellings. By taking the critical incidents identified through the coding process in Chapter Three and using the lens the vantage point provides, the characteristics of the roles of the three story components were brought to the surface. By describing the characteristics of the roles of teacher, learner, and content, the shape of the images that live within each storyline begin to become clear.

Moving out of each incident with this knowledge of the role characteristics, the next step was to see what threads might tie together the stories from different times and different places. This process has led to "naming" the roles of the teacher, learner, and content that are evident among the collective stories. In the novel *Cloudsplitter* (Banks, 1998), the young boy who narrates the story retells his father's perspective on the power of such naming. During trips, moving from one part of the country to another, the father was preoccupied with identifying all the trees, bushes, birds, and flowers along the way. When the boy asked his father why he was spending the time doing so, the father explained, "When we have named a thing we have begun to *see* it" (p. 177).

Chapter Five, "Investigating Patterns," will set out a process for articulating claims built into the roles explored in this chapter. The work from Chapter Three on delineating what "expectations went awry" will be key to undertaking the work on the assertions. That upcoming work will provide subsequent chapters with frameworks for tracing consequences and implications of the assumptions. The final chapters will ask, "What milieu or context gave rise and reinforcement to the assumptions and the challenges?" The book will conclude with an exploration of the "self now thinking about future selves"—a naming of avenues for potential growth as a college teacher that the collective process suggests. Simultaneously moving into and through the details of stories, one seeks metaphorically, as in the Denzin quote that opened the chapter, to remove layers of paint from a portrait; the result, he explains, is that "Something new becomes visible" (1989, p. 81).

5

Exploring Patterns

Stories themselves are saturated with theory.
(Grumet, 1981, p. 124)

I know a young Navajo woman who makes weavings on a large up-
right loom. As she interlaces the horizontal threads through the
vertical threads, her design becomes visible. In Bertha's weaving,
the vertical (warp) threads are mounted first parallel to each other
onto the loom, not unlike the initial telling of stories in Chapter
Two. In Chapter Three, some of those stories were identified for
closer attention; the critical incidents were pulled taut on the loom
of retellings to mark their prominence. In Chapter Four, the texture
of each of these key vertical warp threads was magnified through a
description of the roles of the teacher, learner, and content. In the
weaving process, the horizontal (weft) strands are wound onto a
shuttle which then is pulled through at a right angle between the
vertical warp threads from one side to the other. In the concluding
section of Chapter Four, the roles of teacher, learner, and content
were pulled—like the weft threads through the warp—of the critical incidents. Bertha says that with the addition of each horizontal
thread, a pattern begins to emerge.

In Chapter Five, the patterns, what our telling of the stories
reveals, will begin to come into fuller view. When Bertha's weavings are completed, they can be used in a variety of ways—as wall

hangings, rugs, saddle blankets, or shawls, for example. Chapters Five, Six, and Seven will describe the patterns more fully than is possible by just looking at one thread at a time. Chapter Eight will explore implications of the design for use in professional growth. This chapter continues the work of earlier chapters. It pivots from offering a series of prompts aimed at developing increasingly detailed memories about incidents to a more holistic approach that identifies claims perceived in the critical incidents.

Within the impressions left by the stories on the storyteller are claims (assertions) about the world, as presented by the people and actions in each. In addition to telling some stories for entertainment, we may tell stories for some prescriptive purpose—to teach a lesson, to illustrate a moral in its narrative arc, or to draw an evaluative contrast. In this, we react, agreeing or disagreeing with the assertions within the stories. The further we get from a story itself, the more we take control over how we invite others to see our view. Foregrounding certain details, glossing over others, and expressing the emotions the story engendered when we experienced it make us authors of the story, not just one of its participants. Assertions are a part of the "understory" in most single incidents. Someone in the story, either through their words or actions, claims something, and in our telling of the story, we judge that claim. Through probing the patterns for assertions embedded within the stories and our tellings of them, we can see how they contribute to bringing current, often unacknowledged, assumptions into view.

In the opening pages of *Professing and Pedagogy* (2005), English professor Shari Stenberg tells about a writing prompt to which students were asked to respond: "Describe a teacher" (p. xi). In jotting down her own description, she writes about a fourth-grade teacher. She remembers her as "maternal," a "disciplinarian," someone who was both "caring and nurturing," and someone who "makes sure students remain in line" (p. xi). The teacher had enough of an impact on her that years later, Stenberg brings up the story in her own class. In the retelling, Stenberg implies a claim inherent in the teacher's actions, that a teacher's role is to balance care and control. At a later point in her book, she discusses the value of engaging in an "ongoing dialogue between the pedagogies from which we've learned and the pedagogies we seek to enact" (p. 66).

One of the ways to do this is to take not only *what* we told in earlier chapters—whether done orally, in memory-jogging notes, or in the development of a fuller written narrative—but *how* the "self now" tells the story of the "self then" (Bruner, 1990, p. 121). The process for exploring this is challenging beyond just recounting details as we probe the synthesis of roles developed in the conclusion of Chapter Four. The process now goes *into* that data to see what might come to the fore as we choose to retell the stories years after they happened. This involves new ways of thinking about stories that have accompanied us through our careers in often unacknowledged ways. I approach this stage in looking at my own stories with a measure of curiosity and trepidation.

I could leave the stories as they are—maybe "Students Applaud Students" is simply a story of engaged learning. On the other hand, my sense is that such a story has more to reveal in the interaction between the students and me. I know it is easier for me to tell about "Students Applaud Students" when I describe their actions without acknowledging my role as an obstacle to their accomplishment; there is more to tell than what someone can perceive who merely hears me recount the story. I encourage you to draw on your curiosity about the claims within stories you are working with in this process. Your wonder about how these critical incidents play a role in your career can be a counterpoint to any trepidation that you might find.

Introduction to Articulating Claims

Indelible impressions come to us through the images in stories. In a broad context, a child's daily life is made up of teaching-learning encounters, and a simple example here serves to introduce the way claims can be embedded within those impressions: my dad drove a Pontiac, bought Texaco gas, loved tomato soup from the can, and smoked Chesterfield cigarettes. As a child formulating my world-view, I saw my parents in the center of the universe and could not imagine other people making choices unlike the ones they made. Since my parents, I reasoned, knew everything, hadn't the soup question been settled? From my vantage point at the time, I observed carefully and took each of their choices as claims (assertions): "This is what it means to be an adult." The words and actions in the stories we tell about teaching and learning encounters similarly contain nominations: "This is what it means to be a teacher"; "This is what it means to be a student."

Within critical incidents, some claims are folded into how we incorporate them into our meaning-making. Through words and actions we work at answering key questions for ourselves: "What does it mean to be a teacher?" "What does it mean to be a student?" With the routine of our days and the press of their demands, there are few, if any, moments to think about questions like these. Our actions, however, stand as answers. How do past stories continue to accompany us? And, with what impact? In the stories we tell, we articulate our views of the values inherent in how the participants in the story respond to those questions. Whether or not those story participants *intend* for us to find claims in their words and actions, we view them as such, even if we do not pay them any conscious attention. In the ways we choose to retell stories, we build an internalized blueprint of values through the words and images in our tellings. Whether we view the claims within a story as positive or negative, the critical incidents contributed to the views we have built over time, so, in that sense, our stories and reactions to them are a formative part of our meaning-making.

I know I have told undergraduate education majors at one time or another that a brief junior high school incident taught me something about how not to teach. My seventh-grade science teacher wrote the word "INERT" in capital letters on the board when we failed to understand some fundamental point. He told us, "Use your dictionaries to look it up because under the definition you will find your names." Then the bell rang. He is one of the teachers who taught me how not to respond to students' attempts at learning. Herein is a model of the role of a teacher that in my own teaching, I work to counter.

Similarly, there is another brief story I have told friends when we have gotten into conversations about teachers we have had. In my junior college physics class, the teacher encouraged our persistence as we struggled to understand little cars going up wooden inclines. His patience and encouragement guided us as he helped us untangle our difficulties. I have commented that this is one teacher who taught me something about the role of a teacher that I now try, with varying degrees of success, to emulate. Both of these instances have implicit claims in the stories that became part of a larger story I was constructing about being a teacher. We can find, in claims, images of import: "Stories do work on us, on our minds and hearts, showing us how we might act, who we might become and why" (Sanders, 2000, p. 91).

When I initially faced the stories and my storytelling in these new ways—looking at roles and claims—I found myself struggling a bit to understand what I was seeking and why—maybe in the same way you are. It was a reflection on how and why I used a story as a part of an introduction to a workshop that started me toward a scrutiny of the story and my reasons for telling it.

About ten years ago, I was invited to welcome new college of education faculty to the campus and to lead a workshop on university teaching in our campus context. At the workshop, I elected to introduce myself with the story about the "Shoulder-Shrugger" to accomplish two goals: to entertain the faculty while putting them at ease and to give them a bit of personal background that would balance a generous introduction made by the associate dean. After a few years of being asked to return and repeat the workshop, I began to wonder why that story had such a hold on me that I used it repeatedly as a part of an introduction. I found myself raising related questions: Why this story and not others? Why am I increasingly embedding stories in settings like this? What makes these stories so persistent? And might there be more to these stories than entertainment?

When I thought about the "Shoulder-Shrugger" and the "Students Asked Me to Leave" stories, I noticed some underlying similarities between them. Initially, it did not occur to me to look much beyond a simple recognition that I had changed my teaching practices and that I was aware that the repeated use of the same stories raised questions for me. I only briefly entertained the thought that these stories and others might have much to teach me about my present teacher-self. In spite of my view that these stories were artifacts from the past, I was curious about why they were still hanging around in my head.

Looking back on it, I sensed that such an exploration might be serious work, but I put off approaching it head-on because I was both uncertain and nervous about what I might find. About this time I began to read about autoethnographic methods where researchers investigate their own presence in their research. I initially took refuge in developing a process influenced by autoethnography for looking more deeply at stories in my repertoire. Along the way, I further developed a reluctant curiosity about why and how "Shoulder-Shrugger" and "Students Asked Me to Leave" lived in the shadows of my teaching.

As the process evolved, I used it haltingly, reflectively, taking breaks when I felt unbalanced by what I was finding. At some point, I got beyond the entertainment value of stories and acknowledged that I was influenced by them, emulating some and rejecting others. The key came when I pursued the question of why I was still holding on to the stories. I switched my attention from my reaction to the stories, to the stories themselves. What claims do the stories present?

Throughout this time I continued each year to work with new faculty and added bits and pieces of the reflective process as I encouraged faculty to link their own stories with their pedagogical choices. I admitted to being uneasy when it appeared that a claim made within my stories contradicted my current intentions and when there was the suggestion that such a story might live somewhere beneath my practices. As I built a reflexive process, I was rewarded in this difficult work when my scrutiny led to "aha" moments that provided a glimpse of some significant and still resonant incident. Even the "uh-oh" moments—moments when I judged the incident negatively but realized it still had a hold on me—taught me something, made me more aware of the roots of my classroom work. Both types of moments arising from my search for claims within the stories invited me to get to know myself in new ways that could benefit my teaching and thus student learning. Given all of the emotions that accompany this work, I have to admit that the rewards of it lead me to agree with a character in the Lobel children's book *Fables* (1980), who says, "I love a squall at sea" (p. 8). Locating claims is an initial step in seeking the more profoundly influential assumptions that Chapters Six and Seven will pursue.

As you look at the actions made by the actors in your critical incident, move from your current reaction to the story and what you perceive to be its influence, to the story as it presents itself in your telling of it. The next section of this chapter will provide examples of doing this to help you approach the question, "What stories do my stories leave me with?" In this, you will open the critical incidents even more than you did when you looked at roles. As a consequence, you will lay the groundwork for looking at influential assumptions that can serve as platforms for professional growth.

Locating Claims

The teachers from our stories are a part of an internal conversation we have about how we think about ourselves as teachers and how that influences what we expect from students and ourselves. To understand what the critical incidents contribute to shaping our teaching, it is helpful to articulate our memory of the claims about what a teacher is, what a student is, and what the role of content is within the stories. In a pared-down way, some claims can be gleaned from brief passages in recollections made by professors who are writing about their teaching. Looking at a few of these in order to deduce potential claims can provide an introduction to engaging in the process for delving further into your own stories. The following examples illustrate a pathway from the storyteller's memories to the claims within them; our assumptions are influenced by the bank of claims—and challenges to those claims—made in our critical incidents.

Examples

When Professor Jane Tompkins writes about her career in education (*A Life in School: What the Teacher Learned*, 1996), she includes a chapter on P.S. 98 because "For a long time part of me has wanted to revisit the dark corridor" (p. 8). In this chapter, she introduces incidents that led her to characterize the school in this way. One of the teachers who made an indelible impression on her at P.S. 98 was Miss Toy. Even as a university professor, Tompkins still carries around some of the claims made by how this particular elementary school teacher prescribed the role of the teacher. In a vivid description of the environment created by the force of Miss Toy's presence, Professor Tompkins writes, "We sat in rows and had to keep our mouths zipped shut, backs straight, hands folded in our laps" (p. 16). Even when Tompkins and her fellow classmates wanted to "get on with reading" (p. 16), Miss Toy held to an approach that, to Tompkins, mitigated against this. Miss Toy's definition of what reading meant in first grade as Tompkins recounts it was that, "The teacher stood in front of the room holding a bunch of flash cards and flashed them at us one at a time" (p. 16). As a teacher, she made little room for one particular learner who pleaded silently, "Here I am! See me! Here we all are, raring to go," and recalls that, "all our wild blood and huge desires were funneled into what pleased Miss Toy the most" (p. 16).

In the classroom, Tompkins remembers, Miss Toy's actions belied a number of unarticulated choices. Through her actions, Miss Toy made the choice to model formality, uniformity, propriety, and order. Through the making of those choices, the teacher in Tompkins's memories exemplifies a set of values underlying what, from her view, it means to be a teacher. When Tompkins reflects that "Everything feathery and diaphanous had been clipped from her character long ago, and now her baleful expression served as a reminder that business was business" (p. 17), her words suggest the claims she remembers as being inherent in Miss Toy's classroom choices: "To be a teacher means . . ." However you complete that sentence, you are engaged in pulling inherent assertions (claims) to the surface. "To be a teacher, according to Tompkins's recollection of Miss Toy means . . ." You might have come up with a variation of the phrase, "to be firmly in control." Or, "to be the architect of learning." Or, "to maintain order in content and behavior." The words that Tompkins uses in her recollection interpret the story, and within her interpretation are some of the claims Miss Toy's actions left behind with one of her pupils.

In another example, political science professor Larry Spence recalls the choices a teacher made in creating an environment for young learners that influenced his own pedagogical craftings. Spence's account in "Drill and Practice" (2009) provides another opportunity to tease out claims made within stories. An early schoolroom experience made such an impact on Spence that in his own teaching he sought to utilize the process, but not the approach. His essay illustrates how the influential incidents in our memories can contain claims we integrate into our thinking. In Spence's retelling, his judgment of the teacher's claims about what a teacher is appears as obvious as the teacher's claims themselves: "Hours of impatiently adding six place columns, doing countless division problems, repeating state capitals' names and reciting

Merchant of Venice ruined my life in school . . . The drudgery did not kill my desire to learn, but it did foster disdain toward teachers and school" (p. 5).

You might choose to adopt, adapt, or reject the assertions within your critical incidents. Later in the essay, Spence foreshadows an interpretation that leads to his adaptation of the practice: "Deliberate practice seems daunting. Is it?" (p. 5). He explains how (and why) he adapts the process so it engenders learning rather than the response he had experienced years earlier. The teacher in his memory made choices about what it means to teach. In these choices are assertions that become a part of Spence's own conceptions of teaching. Consider the assertions you see in the brief vignette and complete the sentence: "To be a teacher, according to Spence's recollection of the unnamed teacher, means . . ."

You might have come up with a variation of the phrase "to command repetition," or, "to rely on routine," or, "to seek uniformity." Even in a few sentences, there are a number of possible claims, but the key is which, from the vantage point of the storyteller, were brought forward from that time to this. Using the metaphor of orienteering—a process of searching out a destination within an outdoor environment by using mainly the environmental markers themselves—S. S. Hall (2004) describes the personal kind of mapmaking that we undertake when looking at claims in stories we tell: "The coordinates marking this territory are unique to each individual and lend themselves to a very private kind of cartography" (p. 15).

In one more example of the way claims are made and used, the author of the brief essay "My Best College Teachers" (Jones, 2010) is explicit about the ways four professors became part of how he constructed the map of his teaching. Instead of recounting individual incidents, Jones synthesizes the role of the teacher in much the same way that you were invited to do at the conclusion of Chapter Four. As Jones tells it, these four teachers were "models for what I aspired to be as a college professor" (p. 6). Two sentences provide a glimpse of the assertions that had the profound influence on the then-student who would himself become a college teacher: "My teachers had the uncanny ability to provide opportunities to students to do much more than listen. Through the intricate structure of their lectures, course readings and assignments, and in-class and formal discussions, they guided students up and down a ladder of intellectual skills" (p. 6).

From both the title of the essay and the tone of this brief passage, it is clear that Jones embraced and sought to emulate these teachers, to take their claims about what it means to be a college teacher as his own. In the second part of the essay, though, he describes how he had to move from mimicry to adaptation. "I hoped what my best teachers had used so successfully would work for my students ..." (p. 7). To conclude this introduction to claims, consider the assertions you see in the brief vignette from Jones's essay and complete that sentence. "To be a teacher, according to Jones's recollection of the four teachers means, . . ."

This time you might have to come up with a variation of the phrase "to actively engage the learners," or, "to purposefully shape content." In this example, the storyteller, by virtue of the very title of his essay, judges the claims favorably and draws the line from story through influence to practice.

Summary of Examples

In the examples from Tompkins, Spence, and Jones, the participants in each story send messages about the roles of the teacher, student, and content through their actions. These are starting points for articulating claims because claims are really extensions of a story line. The complexity of claims will be a part of a subsequent teasing out of assumptions in Chapters Six and Seven, so looking for claims about the roles of teacher, student, and content will give you a platform from which to undertake that work. In each story that Tompkins, Spence, and Jones recount, the choices were made from many options, and these choices (with their inherent claims)

are part of what made the incidents memorable to the person recalling the story. The storyteller is the one who shapes the story,
and if prompted to look beneath the story's details, may come to
perceive claims within them and the values they exemplify. The
assertions about what "being a teacher" means and what "being a
student" means have impact in that they are part of stories with
enough influence on the teller to be remembered even years afterwards. Within a bank of memories, the claims in the incidents
can come to be challenged, reiterated, exaggerated, or minimized.
In writing about the power of personal stories in her own life, bell
hooks says, "I like to think I am because the story is" (2010, p. 50).
As the tellers of tales, we are also their authors.

The next section of this chapter invites you to construct a list of
claims within the critical incidents you have identified in Chapter
Three. This list will become the field through which to go (to quote
Brookfield once again) "assumption hunting." In a book suggesting a process, however, it is important to once again reiterate the
significance of your proceeding in personally meaningful ways and
trusting the personal adaptations that you make. By now, you have
probably found a strategy for tracing your reflections through the
two previous stages; you may be using a series of jottings, journal-
type entries, written stories, drawings or diagrams, or interchanges
with colleagues. Continue in this stage to record your explorations
in whatever ways are meaningful for you, and in ways you can continue to refer to in subsequent chapters. As Hall (2004) developed
his orienteering metaphor in the essay cited earlier, he comments
that, like the reflection process we are building, "All maps are the-
matic, personal maps even more so; like everyone else, I lay down
my lines and sail the wobbly grid" (p. 16).

Claims within Critical Incidents

The goal of this next stage is to develop a list of claims you now see
embedded within your critical incidents, messages you perceive as

being sent about the role of the teacher, the role of the student, and the role of content. Without worrying about matching some "right way" to do this work, use the explanations and examples as tools to construct your own way to discover some of the "bones" that hold up the story together in your memory. The result will *not* be a list of statements reflecting all the claims you now embrace. The list of assertions you draw out will be those that, at one time or another, presented themselves to you in incidents that have remained a part of your repertoire of stories.

You might begin this stage with the summary statements at the conclusion of Chapter Four, the synthesized characterizations of the role of the teacher, student, and content. For each of those three, look *into* the synthesis statement, take a metaphorical breath and draw out the claims you sense are there. You could also review your notes, in whatever form you have them, on each critical incident. If you are working with a colleague, he or she might volunteer to listen to your accounts as you tell the stories and then offer to tell you what claims they hear. Taking your colleagues up on this offer to identify assertions, however, can divert you from identifying the claims *you* see. Your colleagues may have insights influenced by their own contexts, which can then be superimposed on your story. But, talking with someone about your summary statements from the end of Chapter Four and the way they relate to your stories from Chapter Three can provide a way to see other details of the stories, and this may make you even more conscious of the messages that live there. On the way to uncovering assumptions, however, the claims you see are the claims *you* see.

As you proceed through this stage, you may become conscious of the extent to which your retelling of the incidents (either to yourself or to others) has shifted over the years since the incidents took place. Intervening experiences and even reflections on the critical incidents influence the way your "self now" sees your "self then." Stories change as we do: "Even when words remain the same, their meanings change as we become different" (Loy, 2010, p. 11).

Realizing this also adds another layer to the way stories live with us as we grow and change in our professional thinking.

The line of action (or plot) in the stories both individually and collectively comes about because of choices we as storytellers recall as being made by others and ourselves. The choices, and the underlying—most often subconscious—values those choices exemplify can give rise to the messages we embed within our retellings without our even being aware of it. A character in one of Alexander McCall Smith's novels (2010) characterizes this line between the past and present as "porous" and says, "Our past is written on us like the lines on a palimpsest or the artist's rough sketch beneath the surface of a painting" (Kindle location 224). This stage of looking for claims etched into critical incidents is challenging because articulating claims in our own stories calls for delving into the role patterns within incidents and across them to articulate constituent parts. It takes scrutiny, it takes patience, it may take walking around, and it may take just letting this slant on the stories sit with you for a while.

Naming the Claims

In whatever way you approach this stage, the intent of the process is to encourage you to color outside of the lines of any prompt so the process fits the emerging design of your own narrative. The process-prompts that follow here are intended to suggest ways of seeing the aspects of the design that emerge from within each story. Going back to the role patterns, revisiting the critical incidents and their claims shifts the process: "Discovery of the deeper issues [that] requires a more holistic approach that can interface with the chaotic and fuzzy realities" (Webster and Mertova, 2007, p. 77). The prompts are not meant to suggest conforming to a rigid structure like the espalier that Larry in a Carol Shields novel describes: "a plant trained on a trellis or a wire. It wants to grow in three dimensions, that's its impulse, but you can flatten it out so it nicely covers a fence or a back wall" (1998, p. 198). Each of the following prompts seeks instead to enable you to value the increasing dimensions of the stories, not to flatten them out. Look for an approach that fits how you are choosing to search through any "fuzzy realities"; in this, let your search be guided by but not restricted to the prompts. A claim is an assertion the characters in the story make through their actions, These actions make visible the role they view should be played by teachers and/or students. As you seek those claims they may seem obvious, maybe obscure, or maybe irrelevant. I encourage you to persist in order to take another step into what stories you recall and how you recall them.

It may be that following the earlier examples in the chapter you have already developed a list of claims because it was easier to link your own examples with the illustrative ones. If you have not yet sought out claims in each of your critical incidents, then here are some guidelines for doing so. Proceed with curiosity and confidence!

This is what it means to be a teacher: What claims do you now see within the pattern for the role of the teacher arising from your critical incidents? Don't stop with the first or second ones that come to mind, but see if more arise as you sit with the role patterns and the stories. If you see one claim easily, look further but know that whether you see one or many, you are doing productive work that will enable insights into what influences your teaching.

This is what it means to be a student: What claims do you now see within the pattern for the role of the learner arising from your critical incidents? Don't stop with the first or second ones that come to mind, but see if more arise as you sit with the role patterns and the stories.

This is what content means in relationship to teaching and/or learning: What claims do you now see for the role of the content arising from your critical incidents? Don't stop with the first or second ones that come to mind, but see if more arise as you sit with the role patterns and the stories.

You might not have considered previously that there were claims being made in any of your stories. After looking at the material you have gathered, it's hard to say how many claims might be in your total list—a half-dozen? a dozen? two dozen? Similarly, it is hard to tell which of the three areas might have the most or least number of assertions, claims about the teacher, the learner, or the content. At this juncture you might find assistance in reading your list to one or more colleagues. In your reading, you will be listening to yourself while speaking so patterns may become visible. Doing this may enable you to see what presents itself in the whole. At some point, you will probably make one or more of these observations. First, you might notice repetition of some assertions even though the words vary; second, you might notice contradictory ideas; third, you might notice some of the claims are those to which you aspire and others are those you work to reject in your own practice; fourth, you—like in the Spence essay—might see that you have adapted some of the claims. These are among the patterns from which you can gain insight into a key question pursued by this work: What is it in my teaching that critical incidents can help me understand? "On the basis of some information and a little bit of guesswork," Toni Morrison writes in "The Site of Memory" (1998), "you journey to a site to see what remains were left behind and to reconstruct the world that these remains imply" (p. 192). Consider that these assertions are memorable enough to be accompanying you on a journey of professional meaning-making. It means that both the stories and our teaching can be considered in new ways. Stories, describes Moon, "can be turned over in the hands, examined from different sides, looked at from underneath or looked at afresh" (2006, p. 125). Looking into our *telling* of stories in these new ways to see what messages are a part of the design present in our memories can lead us to "becoming aware of the implicit assumptions that frame how we think (Brookfield, 1995, p. 2).

Next Steps

With the completion of two stages in this process of critical reflection, the threads in the emerging patterns of influence are present. In Stage One, the recall of stories and coding of our reactions to them led to the identification of critical incidents; in Stage Two, the exploration of details built themes and messages that were most indelibly present in the critical incident themes and stories. When Connelly and Clandinin write that "from the narrative point of view, identities have histories" (1999, p. 95), they suggest that one's narrative roots are linked to the emerging design of assumptions.

If you sense that the line between claims and assumptions is fuzzy, that is because it is. One reason is described in Brookfield's *Becoming a Critically Reflective Teacher* (1995). In the beginning of his book, Brookfield draws attention to three different categories of assumptions: the causal, the prescriptive, and the paradigmatic (pp. 2–3). "We must then," he writes, "try to find a way to work back to the more deeply embedded prescriptive and paradigmatic assumptions we hold" (p. 3). The process in this book has been laid out to make this work possible. In the next step, in Chapters Six and Seven, the distinctions among these layers of assumptions will be laid out and used to get deeper into pedagogical practices.

How do the claims in our telling of critical incidents prefigure different layers of assumptions underlying our work in classrooms? What assumptions guide the theory-in-practice our teaching decisions exemplify? How have assumptions influenced our classroom practices in ways visible and invisible? In what ways do we each personally "scratch a theory" and "find a biography" (Torres, 1998, p. 1)? Stage Three in this work of looking at what our stories teach us will extend the examination of stories to pursue responses to these questions. Whatever insights you have gained from looking at roles and claims, themes and assertions will accompany you.

Whether you are more deeply curious about the links between stories and teaching practices or perhaps are more skeptical that such links can inform professional growth, consider again Madeline Grumet's words that opened this chapter: "Stories themselves are saturated with theory" (1981, p. 124).

6

Locating Assumptions

Does that mean that our autobiographies are
constructed, that they had better be viewed not as a
record of what happened (which is in any case a
nonexistent record), but that rather as a continuing
interpretation and reinterpretation of our experience?
                                    (Bruner, 1994, p. 28)

I opened the class period in a course about introducing graduate teaching assistants to university teaching by announcing the
topic for the afternoon: "Today, we will explore the key features
of how to create the Natural Critical Learning Environment, as
described in Ken Bain's book, *What the Best College Teachers Do*
(2004)." The semester had raced by and I wanted to make sure
they learned about these points from Bain's work. In a 50-minute
class there is really little time, so I rushed to cover material, conscious of both the rapidly approaching end of the period and the
end of the semester. When I saw that 45 minutes had passed, I
gasped—audibly. Students looked up from their note taking. At this
point, I did something I rarely do in a class—I swore. Then I asked
them (and myself), "Did you notice that while I was lecturing on
the value of following the guidelines for setting the Natural Critical Learning Environment, I failed to demonstrate any of the five
components?" They smiled charitably, gathered their materials, and

left class. I was appalled by how I had conducted class: What *is* this contradiction doing smack in the middle of my learner-centered intentions?

I couldn't chalk this up to inexperience or distraction, and my immediate rationales seemed flimsy. Here was a disquieting tension, a moment of disruption and discomfort that echoed others that had sometimes startled me in my teaching. Tensions like these show themselves to me at various times, and usually, in one of three ways: by a challenge of intentions, a contradiction to actions, or a disruption of routines. In the equation, the expected or intended pulls against the actual action, and depending on the context, the resulting tension falls on a continuum from annoying to appalling—even from confirming to constructive. Whatever the nature of the tension, looking closely at it has the potential to be instructive. Stage Three of this book's process of examining critical incidents from our educational biographies focuses on identifying assumptions that feed these moments that catch us off-guard, moments during which we find something going on that challenges our view of the relationship between intentions and actions. As I've become increasingly conscious of some of the assumptions that live in my teaching, I have recognized these moments more as related tensions rather than unrelated, individual occurrences. In the work in this chapter, we are pursuing a response to Loy's question, "What happens when I realize my story is a story?" (2010, p. 33).

Map of Progress and Destination

To this point in the book, the focus has been on the details and designs woven from critical incidents and our tellings of them. Some of the stories may have been told multiple times as we have reminisced over the years about our teaching, or we may have only recently discovered their persistence in our memories in response to the process in this book. Patterns of assertions about our teaching appear within critical incidents. Doing this work is certainly more difficult than trying to recount details of a powerful story. The payoff in working through the difficulty is gaining one's insight into the legacy of critical incidents and how recognition of their unbidden influence can enable a deepened understanding of our current practices.

Chapter One introduced the storied contexts of our work as college teachers—how narratives about school experiences are embedded in everything from our vitaes to the ways in which we construct a course or teach a single class. Chapter Two sought out memorable stories of teaching-learning encounters that emerged in response to a series of prompts. Within this first stage of the process of exploring what our stories teach us, identifying a repertoire of stories with touchstone titles and descriptive details established plumb lines for the subsequent work. Chapter Three introduced a coding process that brought focused attention to some of these stories. As Stage Two proceeded in both Chapters Four and Five, the critical incidents were further developed through recollections of each story's impact. This was followed by an explication of the roles played by teachers, students, and content both within and across the critical incidents, leading to even deeper immersion into the stories. Chapter Five switched attention from the details in the stories to the *telling* of those stories. In this, the messages communicated when critical incidents are told became the focus. Within the telling of the key stories, details highlighted, actions communicated, and lessons learned all became keys to identifying the claims presented and the challenges made.

The process for arriving at this juncture has been guided by a series of suggested prompts. The intent of the prompts has been to frame first breadth and then pursue depth of stories that, surprisingly or not, have remained as key memories long after their genesis.

In Chapters Six and Seven, Stage Three invites us to dig through the stories, details, claims, and challenges to uncover assumptions that are antecedents for our teaching actions.

Within the daily course of my teaching, I can point to some incidents like the one that opened this chapter. What sticks in my mind, however, are only rarely the incidents themselves, but rather, the uneasiness the incidents engender about my teaching. Over coffee, an anthropology professor with a long and successful tenure in college teaching admitted that tensions continue to be a part of her teaching, too. This was an unexpected topic of conversation between two college teachers. More expected would be a trading of classroom incidents—not an acknowledgment that we each recognized patterns of tensions in our teaching between monologic content-delivery with its focus on teaching and dialogic-engagement with its focus on learning.

Critical incidents as identified and pursued in this book represent opportunities to begin the process of investigating the genealogy of those tensions. The question I rhetorically posed to the graduate students, "Did you notice that while I was lecturing... I ignored all of the components?" was hard to pose and painful because the answer to the question was so obvious. Here I was, in the middle of doing what Schön calls *reflection-in-action* (1983), watching myself with a third eye, and seemingly helpless to change the momentum of the class in any way other than saying "damn." Ten years from now, if I was asked to recall pivotal narratives that might reach a threshold of "critical incidents," this story may or may not be one. Today, I see it more as an illustrative anecdote of current tensions in my teaching. It is the intensive explication of critical incidents, akin to Schön's *reflection-on-action*, a more deeply reflexive process that will be pursued through the work in Stage Three. This process seeks to contribute insights beyond a simple acknowledgment of a disruptive action or reaction to something in my teaching.

From Critical Incident to Assumptions

In order to ferret out assumptions, the process in this book uses critical incidents, rather than daily classroom procedural actions (see Tripp, 1993). Because the origin of the process is in what Bruner calls "turning points," these incidents become "steps toward narratorial consciousness" (1991, p. 4). This approach investigates growth from current tensions that arise in teaching. It can be a disconcerting process to move from the rich narratives of critical incidents informed by the claims and the challenges they entail through to assumptions. Doing this leads to taking an unvarnished look at multiple layers of reasons underpinning choices made in our teaching.

Exploring what our stories teach us requires a willingness to be vulnerable and open to new insights that may confirm or challenge our existing beliefs about our identity as teachers. In a book on undertaking critical reflection in the health care field (2011), Rolfe, Jasper, and Freshwater speak to my reluctance to face what I discover: "[I]t is normal and natural to subconsciously or unconsciously protect ourselves from some of the more personally uncomfortable conclusions we may arrive at" (p. 6). As I work through stories from details to interpretation to analysis-for-assumptions, I have done so while sometimes uncovering layers of "personally uncomfortable conclusions." In doing this, I find myself facing aspects of my teaching it would be easier to overlook.

One of the stories that is indelible enough to be a critical incident for me is "First Day," the story of what happened when I was first hired as a teacher in 1969. It is my desire to understand and grow in my teaching that moves me to pursue the work of analysis, even when I find perspectives that surprise me. Although "First Day" is on the list of stories identified earlier in this book, I have not yet told it. I do so here because it illustrates how the process of critical reflection is always an unfinished one, and because through it, my assumptions inherent in this critical incident can be traced.

An Example

After more than a decade of doing this work on stories, I find new artifacts as I move deeper into the critical incidents. Seemingly unbidden, long-forgotten images hidden in memory appear in stories while I am telling them. In "First Day," one of my critical incidents, just such a recent detail startled me into a confirming insight, even as I was drafting this chapter.

First Day

In preparation for my first day of teaching in the late 1960s, I did a dress rehearsal the night before. I was nervous about meeting the eighth graders and tenth graders who would be coming to English class the next morning. A carefully planned wardrobe, I reasoned, would communicate an appropriate image. I picked out a paisley dress which I hoped would make me look older and fashionable three-inch black patent heels to make me look taller, and picked up my new briefcase to make me look smarter. I stared approvingly into the mirror and practiced saying my name.

The next day, with my costume masking my shaky confidence, I walked into the room to prepare my desk before the class arrived. Around three sides of the perimeter of my desktop I built a fence-line of reference books and teacher's editions of texts. I placed my briefcase on the floor next to my desk so it would be clearly visible to entering students. And on the chalkboard I wrote, erased, and rewrote my name until it looked bold and strong-handed enough to satisfy me.

Moments after the bell rang and the students were seated I cleared my throat to begin; the door reopened and one last student entered the room. He stopped halfway between the door and my

desk, looked at his classmates, looked at me, and then approached
my desk. In doing so he walked *around* the barrier of books I had so
carefully constructed, stood next to me, put out his hand to shake
mine, and said, "My name's Ronald and I'm gonna be in your class."

On this first day of my career, for which I had so carefully prepared my teacher-self, Ronald's words and actions said I would do
well to pay more attention to students. This is a story I recount with
vivid details whenever I have an occasion to talk about learner-
centered teaching. In the multi-stage process of analysis, I have
come to recognize the narrative as having significance for me beyond that of an entertaining anecdote (Shadiow, 2009). The additional detail that showed itself—as I have been going through
the same process I am inviting you to do in this book—is that in
this story there was also a large wooden lectern. This is a seemingly
insignificant detail about a piece of furniture that there would be
no need to include in a retelling of the story. This, however, has
been buried beneath the "tectonic layers" which Schlink (1998)
describes as resting "so tightly one on top of the other that we always come up against earlier events in later ones" (p. 217). My recollection of this large wooden lectern in the corner of the room, of
my dragging it center stage that day before students filed in, and of
my tight grasp on its sides as I stood behind it peering over the top,
now gets added to the scene that plays in my head because buried
among these details is an additional, more significant one.

At midyear Ronald and a few of his friends proudly walked into
class one morning with a gift they had made for me in shop class, a
new lectern that was perfectly sized for their 5'2" English teacher.
Assumption-hunting has led me to uncover this image and help me
learn from its newly emerged presence. Their gift of the lectern was
an invitation to reduce the distance between us and an invitation to
care. My recollection of the lecterns, mine and theirs, resoundingly
underscores the claims and challenges I find in the collection of

critical incidents that were discussed in Chapter Five. The contrast between the two vivid images provides me with a reference point for understanding the claims and challenges.

In this "First Day" story, I had totally forgotten about using the lectern to both physically and psychologically steady myself. As I was writing the draft of this chapter an image of a lectern just appeared between sentences. At the moment it did, it brought tears to my eyes because it had been a hidden image that, with its appearance, asks more of me as I try to lay open the critical incidents. The next image, the students proudly presenting me with their lectern, stopped me in amazement at the details that can be unearthed when some of the top layers of stories are moved aside. They could have made me a pencil holder or a trinket box, or nothing at all. But with a lectern, I now read this as an acceptance of who I was at that time in my career and as an acknowledgment that they wanted me to make myself more visible, more accessible to them as we came to trust each other. There were follow-up incidents that now lead me to interpret their gift in this way; my tearful moment when I recovered this image brought back a flood of other incidents that year when the students slowly drew me out from behind the podium.

Part of me wants to leave this story alone now without analyzing it further. "First Day" is a critical incident with tangible and emotional details, with embedded claims about teaching, and with a main narrative unexpectedly countered by students. But, I do not think Ronald is finished with teaching me. I owe him, my students, and myself an even closer look at what this critical incident can reveal. Perhaps you are thinking this process reads too much into these stories—the students built a custom lectern—mine was too tall. They needed a shop project; they were trying to be nice. There's nothing more to it. For many reasons, I believe there is more to it. It is an incident that was pivotal enough to have been a touchstone for me through the years; its "lesson" has influenced the way I think about teaching, and the assumptions I have worked diligently to uncover have helped me to understand and strengthen my teaching today.

Defining Assumptions

Throughout this book, the point has been made that the intricacies of stories are not immediately apparent. Roles, claims, and challenges come into view as the process evolves. Making details evident when one looks *at* a story, looking *into* those details, and then finding what is *beneath* there demands focused attention, but it also requires doing so, usually from a distance. Years of teaching experience have intervened between the time that the lectern was presented to me as a gift and this moment of drawing assumptions from the telling of the story. Now, analyzing the story is like turning the focus mechanism on a pair of binoculars in order to increasingly sharpen the details.

Pratt (1998) discusses the intricate designs of beliefs that build a structure of assumptions. These assumptions, he says, enable interpretation and hold a host of features in place. "Teachers' notions of learners, content, context, and ideals, and what it means to teach" (p. 217) are all held together with the glue of assumptions. By "digging deeper into perspective[s] on teaching" (p. 217), and by "digging back under layers of one's biography" (Grumet, 1981), those undertaking critical reflection are actively seeking insight. Pratt also uses "excavation" to characterize that this "mining" of stories is viewed as necessary to reach the rich vein of assumptions. The thread of mining metaphors in the literature on critical reflection is particularly vivid for me because my father worked in the open-pit iron ore mines in Northern Minnesota's Iron Range.

I have always been fascinated by the process miners use to examine the terrain, move huge amounts of earth to look into that terrain, and then undertake the more arduous work necessary to delve deeper beneath the earth to locate the significant resources that the terrain hid from view. There is richness in recalling memorable incidents, but the richest resources lie in locating assumptions. It does, like iron ore mining, require "heavy lifting."

Three Categories of Assumptions

A number of articles provide reviews of literature on how "assumptions in general are centrally important because they provide the foundation of thought, action, and arguments" (Yancher and Slife, 2004, p. 85, is one such source). Rather than review that literature here, drawing on Brookfield's discussion of three types of assumptions will more easily move this discussion to analysis of the stories. If Stage One in the process of this book is about description, and Stage Two is about interpretation, then Stage Three is about analysis.

In the introductory discussion, subtitled "Reflection as Hunting Assumptions" in *Becoming a Critically Reflective Teacher* (1995), Brookfield defines assumptions as "taken-for-granted beliefs about the world and our place in it" (p. 2). He then calls the realization of our implicit assumptions an "intellectual puzzle." He poses a challenge: "Who wants to clarify and question assumptions she or he has lived by for a substantial period of time, only to find out they don't make sense?" (p. 2). Over the last decade, I have come to answer Brookfield's question: "*I* do." I believe my teaching and the resulting student learning will be strengthened through the difficult task of the sense-making which Brookfield addresses. Gaining an evolving appreciation of my stories (now on multiple levels) is one of the ways in which I have grown to be more accepting of the discomfort that can come from unraveling their messages. I encourage you to suspend your skepticism, if it is part of what you bring to this work at this point. Trust that the presence of long-held stories in your memories are there for reasons besides entertainment. Trust that they continue to accompany you in your teaching for reasons that assumptions can help you learn.

In a few brief paragraphs Brookfield distinguishes among three categories of assumptions (pp. 2–3): causal, prescriptive, and paradigmatic. All three types have influence on our actions, our view and judgment of events, and our choice-making. When something "goes awry," it is likely due to the deeply rooted and deeply held paradigmatic assumptions that are being challenged. This is what influences us when we have to react quickly and rely on what we say are "instincts" or "intuition." Both are profoundly influenced by assumptions, and critical incidents are key places to locate them.

The following brief description of each of the three types incorporates one example of each, and this precedes two other examples, including a look at what assumptions I see currently in "First Day." Through these examples you will have experience looking at this assumption-hunting process in others' stories to assist you in undertaking the process for your own selected critical incidents.

Causal Assumptions

When in our teaching practices we do one thing and are guided by the belief that something will automatically follow, there is a *causal assumption*. Here is a teaching practice and the expectation that combine to form a causal assumption: "If I pose questions and manage the flow of discussions it is because I expect students will then participate in discussion." It is the type of assumption that looking *at* the story makes visible. Our teaching practices are implemented because we think each has the potential to result in an expected response.

Prescriptive Assumptions

Going one layer deeper *into* the details of the incident can reveal a different type of assumption, one where the ideal (and our judgment of something as an ideal) comes to the surface. Looking at the causal assumption and extending it by adding "because I value..." is one way to move to a *prescriptive assumption*. Here is an underlying reason why I make that causal assumption: "By structuring student discussions, I value the student learning that will result."

The reason why I choose the teaching action I do is a signal that I hold the underlying intent as an ideal, a value.

Paradigmatic Assumptions

Paradigmatic assumptions are, as Brookfield defines them, "basic structuring axioms" that lie beneath the story (p. 2). In these underlying belief structures (as Pratt calls them) are rich veins of value that we won't know are there until we move what lies above them. The details of a story belie the depths of their potential meaning. "I choose to structure initiating questions because I expect discussion." "Structuring student discussion is an ideal way to engage their learning, and I value that." "Structuring student discussions is a sign of a good teacher because I fundamentally believe students' learning is dependent on a teacher managing their engagement." You may see other assumptions here, including what may seem like more obvious ones. Sometimes being persistent with asking, "Why is that the case?" at each layer of assumption will enable you to get beneath the topsoil of what is most easily seen.

You may also see more than a single assumption at each of these levels. They are there and are a part of the rich potential for insight, but often, the assumptions at each level will coalesce around one or two key points. With an additional example from "First Day," a story where you have more details than just the one present in this classroom action involving a teacher's role in discussion, this point may become more evident.

Three Assumptions in "First Day"

When I move to look *at* expectations in the critical incident "First Day" (for a causal assumption), then *into* the story for an underlying value (a prescriptive assumption), and then *beneath* that prescriptive assumption (for a paradigmatic assumption), I essentially answer the "why" question for each level. Here are the assumptions I find in "First Day."

As I look *at* the story, I see this *causal assumption*: "My *expectation* is that if I am perceived as older, taller, and smarter, I will be in control."

As I look *into* the story further, I find this *prescriptive assumption* that accompanies this causal assumption: "I *value* being in control as a prerequisite component for teaching."

As I look *beneath* the story and ask "why" I hold the other two assumptions, I find this *paradigmatic assumption*: "In order to learn, I *believe* students need to be led by someone with power. That someone is the teacher."

As I am performing this analysis, I choose the words that unlock each assumption for me. Given the current contexts of my teaching and levels of understanding that I bring to it, I have an "informed lens" that is different from the one I had five years ago—or even one year ago. Rather than choose the more comfortable word "control" in the last assumption, I choose the word "power" as more indicative of the current underlying the incident. In part, I make this choice because I have seen similar patterns in other critical incidents, and I am beginning to take deeper notice of what influences me, even when I have intentions and other practices that counter this one.

Each category of assumption asks me to articulate a reason, and then the next level of assumption asks me to give a reason for that previous reason. Each step startles me into a new level of awareness. And at each level, there is an "aha" moment. The "uh-oh" moments come when I realize that some of my paradigmatic assumptions (like the one in "First Day") contradict some of my current practices (as in both the discussion example used above and the opening story of the graduate class). From these contradictions arise tensions, and I am not likely to recognize the relationship between tensions and assumptions without doing focused and critical reflection.

The ability to locate assumptions is a progressive one, in part because the process can be demanding. Maryellen Weimer's writing draws on her own critical reflection, and she admits that "critical reflection is fine but the process is not always pain free" (2010, p. 30). In my analysis of "First Day," the process leads me to paraphrase words spoken by one of Douglas Adams's characters in *The Hitchhiker's Guide to the Galaxy* (1979): I am only capable of knowing what the state of my current self will allow.

As a reader of "First Day," you might see different assumptions than I do—assumptions that to you seem like more significant ones. You might question what I see or how I represent the points that I do. There are many reasons why this is true. Context counts. As the storyteller and interpreter of the narrative, I bring my own contexts to this work. How I experience an event and then tell about it later are influenced by context. The "self now recalling then" and "the self now interpreting the self then" (Bruner, 1990, p. 121) are both context-dependent. Dialogue with another person may help me to articulate the assumptions I find, but contexts are so personal that asking someone else to formulate my assumptions, particularly paradigmatic ones, is not unlike asking someone else to read my Rorschach inkblot. "A story that is told," writes Denzin (1989), "is never the same story that is heard" (p. 72). The influence of contexts on the assumptions will be explored in Chapter Eight.

Analyzing Incidents for Assumptions

Prior to approaching your incidents to seek out assumptions, here is one more example to assist you in analyzing a story other than your own. English professor Paul Corrigan has a brief contribution to the Commentary section of the journal *College Teaching* that illustrates this process. As you read this paraphrased account, see if you can formulate underlying causal, prescriptive, and possible paradigmatic assumptions.

The title of his essay provides a master key to his story "How I Came to Understand That My Students Would Need Training Wings in Order to Learn to Fly" (2011, pp. 127–128). The details of his essay map directly onto the title. His title skillfully captures the trajectory of his growth: I hold one view about how to prompt student learning; something happened that caused me to reflect on my view; and as a result, I altered assumptions and related teaching practices.

Corrigan opens his essay by speaking of the context of his work, an open-enrollment university, because it situates his story. He writes about setting high learning goals and giving students open-ended choices for determining how they were to fulfill assignments. In choosing to present class material in this way, he expected student learning would result (a causal assumption). As a reader, I see that he answers the question, "Why do you expect that?" He highlights a value—prescriptive assumption—when he answers this "why" question. He explains that he values the unequivocal responsibility teachers have to make student learning possible (p. 127).

Within the article he comments that his practices, expectations, and values (thus the causal and prescriptive assumptions) come from a number of sources. Their foundations are based on how he learned when he was a student: "I took learning into my own hands and ran with it" (p. 127). It is likely that if asked to identify critical incidents, his repertoire of stories would illustrate this.

The challenge to his causal and prescriptive assumptions (you can see claims embedded in each) came as a "rude awakening" (p. 127). In addressing this tension he drew on "reflection, dialogue with colleagues, and reading" (p. 127) and that led him to reconsider his practices. In these reconsiderations he was dealing with his causal and prescriptive assumptions. Before he moves into talking about his changed classroom practices he identifies his altered prescriptive assumption: he values it when students can learn to do intellectual work *with significant support and under conditions that are developmentally appropriate* (p. 127, italics in the original). This shift in his prescriptive assumption results in a related shift in his pedagogical practices, and he describes these in the second part of his essay.

Gleaning his paradigmatic assumptions is problematic. I know little about the personal contexts he brings to telling this story (except that he is a professor who learned through self-direction) or about the context of the story itself (it is an English class in an open-enrollment university). From the two prescriptive assumptions, his original one and his revised one, I do get a sense that a fundamental principle, and thus a paradigmatic assumption, in his teaching is that *most students can learn*. Considering the manner in which he weaves the slim amount of contextual information into the essay, I sense that another paradigmatic assumption embedded in his account could be that *teaching in the way one has successfully learned will lead to student success in their learning*. If he were to inquire further into a reason for his tension (what he calls his "rude awakening"), it is this second paradigmatic assumption that he might discover was being challenged.

Assumptions within Corrigan's Story:

Causal Assumption—looking *at* the story: If I give students open choices, I expect they will use that freedom to learn.

Prescriptive Assumption—looking *into* the story: I expect this because I value the unequivocal responsibility teachers have to make student learning possible.

Paradigmatic Assumption—looking *beneath* the story: I believe teaching in the way one has successfully learned will lead most students to learn.

Working with a collection of stories rather than a single one would enable us to test out the presence and influence of these potential paradigmatic assumptions. Tensions within our teaching can come when something arises that pushes against underlying belief structures. The result, like in Corrigan's account, may lead to a reconsideration of one or more assumptions. Paying attention to related paradigmatic assumptions can lead to more enduring insights and growth. Asking "What unsettled me here?" can begin the process of naming the tensions and then untying those knots in your teaching.

Among the ways of coming to an understanding of these levels of assumptions is to begin with a teaching action you see in a colleague or a teaching action described in a recommended journal article or book on teaching. Even a suggested teaching technique carries with it a set of assumptions that usually go unacknowledged. The 2007 collection *Start With a Story: The Case Study Method of Teaching College Science* (Herreid, 2007) has a series of assumptions nested even within the title. Without going into the expectations, values, and beliefs that the author himself addresses in the introduction and first story in his book, imagine you wrote the book and explore the assumptions that answer the question "why?"

Embedded in the journal essay title "Using Humor in the College Classroom to Enhance Teaching Effectiveness in 'Dread Courses'" (Kher, Molstad, and Donahue, 1999) are another set of assumptions around a certain type of technique being used in a particular context with a specific expectation. Again, ask why such an approach is viewed as desirable as though you are the faculty member who advocates for it in your own teaching. Consider your initial response (an expectation) and then ask "why" to get at the deeper reason that points to some value. Then, one more time, ask "why" to see if there is a belief beneath the value. You may try out going to an additional level of "why" after formulating what appears to be a paradigmatic assumption to see if another one becomes visible.

Where Assumptions Live

In previous chapters you completed the background work that will lead to discovering assumptions in your own stories. By identifying stories, naming them, coding them, and by examining the roles played by the commonplaces within and across stories, you have all of the details needed to help you find what causal and prescriptive assumptions live within your critical incidents. Begin by selecting one critical incident and then identify an initiating action in that incident.

Select a critical incident where you are in a teaching role from among those in the repertoire you have been working with. Selecting a story rooted in your own teaching is a helpful beginning because those incidents can be where insights can more likely be traced. You may find that starting with an incident from your own classroom can later on provide a template for work with other critical incidents.

Identify an initiating action in the incident. In "First Day," the initiating action was my undertaking a dress rehearsal for the first day of teaching. In Corrigan's story the initiating action was his giving students open-ended assignments.

In whatever way works for you, steep yourself in the details you have collected for the incident. You might directly or indirectly use the name, the details, the codes, the roles, and the vantage point in order to remind yourself about the multiple dimensions of the story. Looking through your notes, reflecting on or talking about the incident will bring it back into a rich focus that will enable one or more causal assumptions to become visible. It will be easier initially to begin by identifying one assumption for each category as you go through this process the first time. Doing so will enable you to either add more per incident or move on to other critical incidents with the same process.

Causal Assumptions: *In order to locate a causal assumption, proceed by looking at the story and asking why the incident's initiating action was undertaken: What is it that you expected? Ask, "What response or action did I expect would follow this action?" It might help to use the equation, "When this was undertaken. . . then I expected this to follow . . ." If this approach does not feel like an easy fit for the incident that you have selected, make whatever changes can assist you in formulating a causal assumption.*

The causal assumptions you see in your critical incident may seem so obvious that you do not need to articulate them. No matter how obvious they may seem, putting them into words gives your teaching a visibility and a transparency that makes the subsequent steps possible. An observer brings different personal and professional contexts to their expectations, so what is obvious to the person undertaking the action may differ from what the observer thinks will result. One way to take this into account is to imagine a new professor visiting a class you are teaching. This colleague observes something in class and then asks you, "Why did you do that? What did you expect to happen because you did that?" This action-inquiry-reason dialogue would help your colleague begin to understand one aspect of your teaching.

To move a step further and identify prescriptive assumptions in the critical incident, it is necessary to again take all of the narrative data into account. Having reviewed it either through thoughts or notes, you now have far more than a memorable or entertaining anecdote. Through doing this level of awareness with critical incidents, the realization becomes clear that "narrative operates to deepen, complicate, and even dismantle our settled beliefs" (Gunn, 1982, p. 35). Imagine again that the new professor continues the dialogue after observing a class you are teaching. When you have indicated what you expected would follow a particular action (the action your critical incident includes), your colleague once again asks a "why" question, and "What do you value?" that led you to expect that.

Prescriptive Assumptions: *In order to uncover a prescriptive assumption, proceed by looking into the story asking what influenced your citing the expectation you did. What value do you hold that provided the basis for the expectation*—the causal assumption? Ask, "If I look into this story and the expectation I brought to it, what value do I hold that undergirds this expectation?" Because this is your reading of your own story, use this suggested approach as a guide rather than a directive. Do what will assist you in articulating a prescriptive assumption.

The prescriptive assumptions uncovered in a critical incident are in the shadow of causal assumptions. This book opened with a quote from Norman Maclean's *A River Runs Through It and Other Stories* (1976, p. 92) that speaks to the inter-relationship. He says that "seeing something noticeable" (like a causal assumption) "makes you see something that you weren't noticing" (like a pre-scriptive assumption). How both categories of assumptions help you to "see something that isn't even visible," like a paradigmatic assumption, will follow in Chapter Seven.

Next Steps

The next step is to take a walk, or a nap, or put this work aside for a bit in whatever way will help you regain your balance. This part of the critical reflection process asks for a great deal of close attention, and breaks in that attention make additional discoveries possible. Australian professor Helen Hickson wrote an essay on her own process of reflection on her university work (2011). In it, she explains that the experience is one that requires interludes of solitude: "I needed time away from the busyness of work to think about my assumptions and to allow space for new ideas to emerge" (p. 835). As you have seen, assumptions emerge from purposeful scrutiny of critical events, and the process is fed by taking time for reflection.

Over the years, I have increased my repertoire of pedagogical choices, and I have more skill in drawing on and implementing those choices in teaching. This chapter opened with a brief account of a recent class period where my action contradicted what I espoused. I asked, "Why am I lecturing when I strongly intend to be learner-centered?" "What *is* this tension doing smack in the middle of my intentions?" I returned to the next class with Bain's characteristics of a Natural Critical Learning Environment embedded in the session's focus of study. Near the end of this class, I then pointed out this structure, and we shared a laugh at how different the two class periods were and what the impact was on their learning. Increased confidence and pedagogical agility, however, have made it more difficult to expose the underpinnings of procedural choice-making within my teaching; such an activity seems unnecessary for reasons that Schön (1983) addresses. He reflects that as knowledge-in-action becomes more regularized, the ability to move into reflection-on-action becomes more challenging. For a long time it did not occur to me that reflection on assumptions could bring an understanding of contradictions between what I espoused and what I did. Critical reflection enables a more authentic alignment between what I do and what I intend to do—and what the structural foundations enable and constrain for both.

Reflecting on the causal assumptions (expectations) and prescriptive assumptions (related values) in critical incidents helps me to see where contradictions like the one in the graduate class begin. But, as Jordan writes in her novel *Mudbound*, "Beginnings [are] elusive things. Just when you think you have a hold of one, you look back and see another, earlier beginning, and an earlier one before that. . . [there is] the problem of antecedents" (Jordan, 2008, p. 98). Mining paradigmatic assumptions brings to the surface an even deeper view of the origins and legacies of tensions. The process for excavation of paradigmatic assumptions, the contexts of these assumptions and our recognition of them, and the links between assumptions and current tensions in our teaching will be undertaken in Chapter Seven. Chapter Eight will extend this work to pursue the implications of looking at what our stories teach us for our professional growth. "The benefit," Cortazzi says, "consists in the critical reflection on those experiences to understand what principles and patterns have been at work in one's educational life" (1993, p. 13).

Do not underestimate the power of taking a walk before continuing.

7

Exploring Paradigmatic Assumptions

... quicksilver spills across the charted systems
(Rich, 1978, p. 31)

After all of these years, there is a familiar rhythm in my teaching. Braided throughout any course I teach, there are opportunities for small group work, for reflective writing, for fieldwork, and for student assignment choices. The content and the contexts of each course influence the degree to which these features are present in a class. In many ways they are a part of a "charted system" in my current pedagogy. Even though I implement these features with a conviction about their efficacy, in practice, there is no uniformity in the results; I am never certain that the results will be what I intend. As I reflect critically on my teaching, I have become aware of the expectations, values, and underlying beliefs that provide the philosophic footings for these pedagogical choices. Sometimes, I find the assumptions are like the quicksilver in the line from the Adrienne Rich poem that opens this chapter; they spill in unpredictable ways across the charted systems of my teaching and point to new insights.

A break, whether a walk or another way of moving away from the work like that suggested at the conclusion of Chapter Six, can contribute to the contemplation of assumptions rather than diminish it. In his January 21, 1853, journal entry, Thoreau observes that "Silence is worthy to be heard / Silence is of various depths and fertility like soil" (Sattlemeyer, 1997, p. 448). And, if in that silence you found that there was only more silence, then the break has not been wholly unproductive. Trust that it still makes a contribution to moving toward discovering the mercurial quicksilver of assumptions that will continue to be pursued in this chapter.

In Chapter Six, causal and prescriptive assumptions were sought for a single critical incident with which you chose to work. This chapter will enable you to continue that work with other incidents or to initiate that work if you have not yet done so. Discussions and more examples of these two categories of assumptions will seek to strengthen the groundwork for moving to the less visible, more fundamentally influential paradigmatic assumptions. Among the reasons for exploring these in critical incidents is that they are so deeply rooted that they provide largely subconscious frameworks for our actions. One of the ways the paradigmatic (or framing) structures are a part of our teaching practices is in their unseen influence. This invisibility can come into view when, as in the example that follows, intentions and actions contradict each other.

In the graduate class anecdote with which I opened Chapter Six, I had intentions of utilizing an interactive lecture format to introduce the Natural Critical Learning Environment in Ken Bain's work (2004). Instead, I bulldozed through the material with no opportunities for student engagement. At the conclusion of class I recognized the contradiction between my intention and my actions. As with other contradictions that show themselves in my teaching, I characterize these as tensions. Yes, I had a rationale for my classroom approach (time was short, students were attentive, I was on a roll), but the rationale didn't help me with the uneasiness I felt when I became aware of the contradictions. Without deliberate attention to critical reflection, I would not be likely to know about or understand the influence of assumptions on my teaching. So, work on unearthing those assumptions from critical incidents can make a contribution to gaining insights into the tensions that may or may not be visible to us. In understanding the intersection between practices and assumptions, though, we can more systematically reflect on and grow in our teaching.

In his 1995 Nobel lecture, literature laureate Seamus Heaney observes, "we are all hunters and gatherers of values." Although he is making a point about how poetry can enable this, I think the same can be said about contemplating the relationship between critical incidents and the assumptions they both reflect and feed. The hunting and gathering Heaney's lecture addresses describes the process this book pursues. On the way to exploring the professional assumptions and their accompanying values about teaching and learning, we are engaged in both "gathering" and "hunting."

The goal of this book is to gather influential incidents from our teaching and learning biographies and then hunt for patterns, assertions, and assumptions in order to grasp their influence on our current teaching practices, both confirmatory and contradictory.

The stages of the process outlined in this book are meant to bring story details alongside assumptions. Stage One (Chapters Two and Three) was the stage of gathering stories and critical incidents; Stage Two (Chapters Four and Five) moved to seeking roles, themes, and claims; Stage Three (Chapters Six and Seven) involves locating three layers of assumptions. The critical incidents identified in the first stage are the primary source for this process. As suggested in this book, your stories, your voice, and your variations of the process now make it possible to consider what knowledge of assumptions will contribute to growing in our teaching.

Through moving from articulating causal and prescriptive assumptions to seeking paradigmatic ones, additional views emerge of the critical incidents we have now grown accustomed to considering in our repertoire. The paradigmatic assumptions are present below the surface of our immediate purview, and multiple examples in this chapter will illustrate that. They are echoed in the choices we make as we do our work whether we recognize them or not. Be patient with yourself as you seek out assumptions from your critical incidents. Assumptions are located within our teaching practices, but it takes patience and persistence to find them there and to take stock of their shape and character in order to discover their presence in our teaching.

Interactions among Categories of Assumptions

The "First Day" story woven into Chapter Six gives an example of two contrasting paradigmatic (baseline) assumptions that provide an introductory, applied definition of the term. In this story, Ronald's actions and mine sprang from two different sets of paradigmatic assumptions about the relationship between students and teacher. The words and actions in our exchange show that difference. Ronald approached me as one person might approach another at an informal gathering rather than the more formal opening of school: "Hi, my name is Ronald, and I'm gonna be in your class." I assumed that in a classroom the opening lines needed to be mine: "Good morning, Class. My name is Mrs. Shadiow, and I'm your teacher." Two dozen words—his and mine. Each represents a fundamentally different way of viewing the world in a classroom.

The word *paradigm* was first used, according to the *Oxford English Dictionary*, in 1483. But its contemporary meaning, a model underlying theories and practices, is credited to Thomas Kuhn's 1962 book, *The Structure of Scientific Revolutions*. Combining a form of the word *paradigm* with the word *assumption* (and its colloquial understanding as something which is taken for granted), *paradigmatic assumption* in this book addresses educational practices. The two-word combination refers to beliefs built into an underlying framework that tacitly influences professional decision making. Whereas causal (expectations) and prescriptive (related value) assumptions are linked to paradigmatic (framing) assumptions, the latter springs from a deeper place in our worldview of teaching. Because of this, the third category of assumptions is so embedded that it is the least easily articulated. This definition can be illustrated in an unlikely place.

Ruth Brown's children's picture book *If At First You Do Not See* (1982) implicitly asks a question about what one can do if a search for meaning appears to be fruitless. How can we respond to that question in our search for paradigmatic assumptions? What might we do if at first we do not see? Brown's book displays a process that applies here. Each of her pages has a few sentences of a story with a colorful illustration. When the pages of the book are turned upside down a second illustration comes into view. For instance, when the cover of the book is rotated, the picture of a butterfly becomes a picture of a cat. Like assumptions, they are not recognized all at once, and they are not static. The very same drawing and colored forms that gave the butterfly shape, when viewed in another way, shift shape and meaning. It is not always easy in Brown's book to see the hidden features, but with each page it becomes easier to puzzle through the upside-down illustrations. Articulating assumptions involves looking at stories in new ways and with each insight, additional insights become possible.

Turning the critical incidents upside down, inside out, and backwards—with patience and intent—causal, prescriptive, and paradigmatic assumptions can be found. Because of all of the notes gathered so far in whatever format has suited you, there is material through which to search. There were insights to be found in the roles identified within and across stories. Applying codes to stories and explicating those codes with "because" statements brought some surprises. You may have sensed some interplay here, some themes threaded throughout these and other constituent parts of the process. Examples in this chapter will illustrate the relationships among the elements, and the themes that you may have sensed are present will lead to tracing paradigmatic patterns. When turning the material in new ways, considering different angles from which to view the collection of details, what is most immediately obscure may be drawn out. To this point, the critical incidents themselves have been the impetus for each subsequent step. Using roles, or point-of-view, or claims as the entry points for the discussion of assumptions (or critical incidents) each brings different possibilities if at first you do not see.

Even though the categories of causal and prescriptive assumptions were introduced in Chapter Six, paradigmatic assumptions are best seen in relationship to these other two categories. The three categories were not addressed collectively in the previous chapter because with more focused and extended attention on paradigmatic assumptions their presence will be easier to uncover. Prior to suggesting a process for delving into the territory of paradigmatic assumptions that underlie critical incidents, the next section will illustrate the relationships among the three categories. It is intended to assist you in clarifying causal and prescriptive assumptions further so paradigmatic assumptions can more clearly emerge in relationship to them. Move through this as slowly or as quickly as is productive for you. If you have yet to identify any causal or prescriptive assumptions, these explanations and examples augment the material in Chapter Six to assist you. If you have identified one or more assumptions in a single critical incident, use this reiteration to revisit that work and then to move on to other critical incidents. What follows is a brief reiteration of the key points for each of these as well as two additional examples.

Reviewing Causal and Prescriptive Assumptions

Causal assumptions are the reasons we take the actions we do—the expectations we have of what will follow a teaching action such as the distribution of an outline of lecture notes to students. "What do I *expect* will happen when I provide students with a set of lecture outlines prior to the lecture?" I have been in conversations with faculty who say they would never use a strategy of providing lecture notes to students prior to the presentation of material. In one respect, their viewpoint and the view of someone who does spring from different sets of assumptions. Like Ronald's and my approach to the first day of school, the perspectives diverge. Even different faculty who use the same practice of distributing notes may respond differently to the question of expectations. Being asked the question (whether of ourselves or by someone else) provides the opportunity for the expectations to be explicit: "I *expect* students will take better notes"; "I *expect* students will be more involved in class." At this most visible level we look at the action and seek to put its intent into words. In this process, attention is drawn to causal assumptions.

Prescriptive assumptions arise primarily by looking into the expectations that surface as causal assumptions. After looking collectively or singly into causal assumptions, the next question is, "*Why* do I hold those expectations for that action?" or, "Why do I believe those expectations have merit?" In the example of providing lecture outlines for students prior to class, there are many possible ways in which an individual faculty member might respond. Here is one prescriptive assumption that the faculty member who has articulated the causal assumptions above might respond with: "I expect students will take better notes because I value their need for assistance with the organization of new material." The causal and prescriptive assumptions may or may not be paired one-for-one. There may be two or three causal assumptions that share a single prescriptive one. The key here is that the prescriptive assumption comes from a different level of scrutiny; they are not as easily recognized as causal assumptions. Prescriptive assumptions can become visible when writing a teaching statement for annual review or when developing a teaching philosophy statement because both actions ask for more than an account of *what* is done in the classroom. Causal and prescriptive assumptions can also be seen when we are reflecting on our teaching in something as informal as a personal journal or as formal as part of an essay meant for submission to a professional publication. But on a day-to-day basis, the prescriptive assumptions get little attention because they demand a deeper level of recognition.

Here is a view of the interrelationships found between the two categories of assumptions:

Causal Assumptions: Looking at the story, what *expectation* accompanies the main action in that story? Causal assumptions are the most evident in critical incidents.

Prescriptive Assumptions: Looking into the causal assumption, what is the *value* that accompanies the causal assumption? Why does the causal assumption have merit? Prescriptive assumptions are implied by the causal assumptions, but they are most often left unsaid unless a question or task prompts their articulation.

Examples

In the literature in which faculty publish essays about their teaching (in publications like *Teaching Sociology, Journal of Engineering Education, Journal of Geoscience Education, College Teaching, College English*, and many others), a close reader can often find these two categories of assumptions addressed in opening paragraphs where directions are set out for the articles. Here are two examples from divergent fields. In the first example, Lewis and Lewis, writing in the *Journal of Chemical Education* (2005), explain in their introductory paragraphs of their article "Departing from Lectures: An Evaluation of a Peer-Led Guided Inquiry Alternative" why they undertook this study. They write that they undertook the teaching reform because they expected that peer-led work *would result in more student-to-student interaction* (p. 135) (paraphrase and italics are mine), a causal assumption. This causal assumption is followed by a description of how they set up the classroom approach and their research study. In this, the prescriptive assumption is present (paraphrase and italics are mine): *student-to-student interactions influence student learning in positive ways* (p. 135). As the authors describe what led to their research study and how they undertook that pursuit, they frame the essay by responding to the unseen questions—first, "What expectations did you bring to implementation of the classroom practice?" and then, "Why do you believe the expectation has merit?" Even though this is a research study rather than a personal essay, there are assumptions present and a story to be told.

Within the second example from the field of sociology, Edwards, writing in *College Teaching* (2007), addresses "Student Self-Grading in Social Statistics." In response to the implied question that can lead to a causal assumption, "What expectations did you bring to the implementation of the classroom practice?" the author explicitly says that the expectation is "*to shorten the turnaround time on homework and tests*" (p. 72), a causal assumption (italics mine). Then again, in response to a second but unstated question, "Why do you believe the expectation has merit?" the author explains that she believes *delays in feedback to students hamper learning* (p. 72), a prescriptive assumption (italics mine). Further implied as another prescriptive assumption is that *feedback from* either *peers or faculty can contribute to learning* (italics mine).

You may find assistance for your work on identifying these two categories of assumptions by picking up a professional journal and reading the first few paragraphs in an article. Draw on either a research report or a personal essay, and look for causal and prescriptive assumptions. The initial discussions of professional articles provide background where implied or directly stated assumptions are a part of the introductory material. As you read, ask what expectation and what values led to the decisions to undertake the work.

As evidenced by the examples from the professional journals, the contexts we bring to any analysis affect that analysis; there are a myriad of ways to express what we sense is present. Working further with your own stories will draw from all of the insights you have gained so far through your reflections. The contexts you bring to this work mean that your words and images are shaped through those lenses. If you are working with colleagues at this stage, they may serve as a helpful sounding board for your ideas, but your own understandings and contexts make you the author. Before moving to paradigmatic assumptions, here is another opportunity to seek causal and prescriptive assumptions within the layers of your own work.

Looking Further into Critical Incidents

In the reflection undertaken in Chapter Six, you were invited to select one critical incident from which to seek one or more causal and prescriptive assumptions. With this brief review of the two categories, it would be helpful to now go back to those assumptions and review them. See if any other assumptions become apparent for that one incident. If you have not yet identified causal or prescriptive assumptions, I invite you to use this opportunity to begin. Either way, trust what you know and feel about the content of these stories that have been with you for a long time. Paradigmatic assumptions are generally going to be evident across multiple incidents and not just in any single story, so moving through each of the critical incidents to articulate the first two categories of assumptions will put key pieces into place for proceeding. Be as simple or as comprehensive as you believe will be useful to you in locating the assumptions your stories present. The goal is to explore two levels of assumptions present in more of your critical incidents. Then, the collection of assumptions will enable undertaking a search for paradigmatic assumptions that are present at deeper levels of analysis.

> Select a critical incident other than the one you worked with in the previous chapter. Review whatever notes you have collected in order to get a three-dimensional sense of the story. Look at an action that is key to the direction of the incident. Then, seek to articulate one or more causal assumptions. Using a form of this question may assist: "What did I expect would happen when this action was undertaken?"

In identifying one or more causal assumptions, you may feel that doing so states the obvious. Because these are a part of a taken-for-granted rationale, this is an understandable reaction, but one that may hinder deeper levels of critical reflection, so I encourage you to persist. You may feel that for the incident you have chosen to work with that assumption hunting does not "fit" the incident. I encourage you not to give up prematurely; using your sense of the incident, address your expectations as a part of your role in that incident—what expectations did you bring to what you did or what you observed being done? If this process still seems too contrived for the incident you have selected, move on to another story. The insights can come more readily as you gain experience in articulating assumptions, so that it may prove fruitful to return later to that incident. You may see one causal assumption or more than that. Because these are your stories and because you are reflecting on your own educational biography, feel comfortable with however many causal assumptions you identify for a story.

For the same story you have just considered in identifying one or more causal assumptions, use the assumptions to move into the story by further taking the additional step of seeking one or more prescriptive assumptions.

> After identifying causal assumptions for one critical incident, ask a form of the following questions to see what prescriptive assumptions have influenced them: "What is the value that accompanies the causal assumption?" "Why do I believe those expectations have merit?" Consider beginning your response with "because . . ." as a way to lead into the prescriptive assumption. You may be doing this in writing, in your head, or in dialogue with colleagues. However you proceed, identifying this layer of assumptions will enable going even further into the rich area of assumptions that influence your current pedagogical work. If the lead-in question is not a good fit, adjust it so it serves your purpose of getting into the values that undergird the expectations. As with causal assumptions, you may find more than one. Rather than

seeking to be exhaustive, identify what resonates with you as it links
to the other assumptions. There is no "magic" number—what is it that
helps you put underlying values into words?

Looking at incidents from your educational biography in these
ways requires adopting a new perspective. It is like "going to the
balcony" to watch the stories unfold below, but with an observer's
rather than a participant's eye. Searby and Tripses use this image
as key to describe their experiences in an essay titled "Going to
the Balcony: Two Professors Reflect and Examine Their Pedagogy"
(2011). They explicitly express two causal assumptions at the beginning of the piece. They explain that they undertook this process
because they expected "to get a new perspective" and "to better understand where we've been, where we are, and where we want to go
with the work in our classrooms" (p. 2). They point to a related
prescriptive assumption when they write that they "value ... taking time to reflect on the effectiveness of our teaching practices,
especially when we sense the teaching and learning processes have
become stale" (p. 1). There are many details to observe in a story,
and many ways to conceptualize those observations. Trust your role
as the interpreter, and trust what resonates with you as you proceed
with other stories. Identify one or more assumptions what would
enable you, like Searby and Tripses, to communicate two layers of
reasons for the actions in each critical incident.

Once you have worked with one critical incident in formulating causal
and prescriptive assumptions, move to the others. First, seek out the
causal assumptions and then, based on those, identify prescriptive
assumptions for your remaining critical incidents.

Whether you have pursued the causal and prescriptive assumptions independently or with one or more colleagues with whom you
can discuss them, making the actions transparent in the stories may
give you much food for thought. When I am engaged in the "doing"

of teaching, the reasons *for* the doing go unexpressed, if I consider them at all. My teaching is not just about technique; it prizes the impact of teaching actions on student learning. Moving to these levels of reflection helps me be a student of my own teaching, and the food for thought nourishes my growth.

Seeking Paradigmatic Assumptions

When Searby and Tripses reported in detail about the nature and consequences of their "going to the balcony," a deeper paradigmatic assumption is implied as a part of the story. The impetus for Searby and Tripses undertaking this reflection was that they were surprised and disappointed by learning from student surveys that a teaching methodology did not have the lasting impact they had assumed would result. They were drawn to use a systematic approach to reflection in order to address this disparity. As was pointed out earlier in their account of the process to resolve this tension, they included explicit expressions of what can be labeled as causal and prescriptive assumptions. As I read their essay describing how they used reflection both for their own growth and for student growth, I saw this emerging paradigmatic assumption: "Intentional reflection is a prerequisite for transformational learning" (meaning for both faculty and for students). Throughout their eight-page essay and the accompanying appendices that are the resulting student assignments, this deeper assumption appears to be the unstated, taken-for-granted belief. This paradigmatic assumption, which they imply they held before this incident, underlies their response to the dissonance they discovered between the intent and impact of their practices. Confirmed by their experiences, the assumption is likely to become even more deeply embedded.

By way of introduction to seeking paradigmatic assumptions, here are the three layers of assumptions I see in the "First Day" critical incident that focuses on my relationship with Ronald and his classmates. Through my current analysis of the incident I see the following:

Causal: When I prepared for class, I did so because my *expectation* was that in communicating a strictly crafted persona, I would be in control.

Prescriptive: Given my expectation, I *valued* the role that control played in the relationship between teacher and students and the achievement of learning.

Paradigmatic: Underlying the other assumptions is the fundamental *belief* that in order to learn, students need to be led by someone with power.

With this third category of assumptions is a belief that is fundamental to and inherent in the first two categories. Paradigmatic assumptions are more difficult to uncover because they are the taken-for-granted components in the way we "know the world" of teaching and learning.

Although paradigmatic assumptions are woven inextricably through professional perspectives and practices, they are obscured by this taken-for-granted nature. Working through causal and prescriptive assumptions may be enough for you at this point in your reflection on teaching. Moving to articulating paradigmatic assumptions, however, will augment the insights you have gathered from critical incidents and add information useful for considering ways to understand the currents flowing beneath your teaching.

Do not let the difficulty be a stumbling block. If it presents what seems like a significant challenge, think of it as a speed bump that is best approached by shifting gears and slowing down. Our stories do tell us a great deal, but it takes a while to quiet the environments so critical incidents can speak on multiple levels. Becoming conscious that there *are* paradigmatic assumptions that provide an underlying structure for our advocacy of some teaching practices and the rejection of others may enable the difficult work on thinking about their presence to begin.

Select one of the critical incidents for which you now have at least one assumption in each of the first two categories. Since each of your stories rose to the threshold of a critical incident, any of them will be a good place to start. Look at the assumptions for that incident and consider a broad belief in which of those assumptions are grounded. Asking this question may assist: "What underlying belief is inherent and embedded in the assumptions that relate to the critical incident?"

When you scrutinize your stories in this way with the goal of putting into words what may seem like being beyond words, you are going to complicate rather than simplify your stories. Do not let what you find in those complications deter you because our stories can reach us at new levels with a power to guide our understanding of our teaching. There are four observations that while contributing to the complications also make the process productive.

First, the same paradigmatic assumptions may be evident in more than one incident. Because these are each stories that you have found in seeking critical incidents (as opposed to entertaining anecdotes), they are likely tied to each other in some unexamined way in your memory. The paradigmatic assumptions in "First Day" and in "Shoulder-Shrugger" both have themes related to my belief in the necessity of using power and control to engage learners in learning.

Second, you may feel that the assumptions that have come to the surface articulate only *some* elements of your deepest framework today. The process of analyzing critical incidents is not meant to be comprehensive. It is meant to begin to unearth significant aspects of an educational biography and to initiate deeper reflection on other stories. As I work through another critical incident like "Students Applaud Students," I unearth a strong belief (paradigmatic assumption) about the necessity of my holding an unquestioned position of expertise as a prerequisite to student learning. Upon further reflection, I see aspects of this embedded in the other critical incidents, too.

Third, you may find some assumptions contradict others you believe currently guide your practice. In constructing this genealogy of growth, the past can illuminate the present and influence the future. Today, after years of having classroom experiences, reading research, and participating in professional development opportunities, I find that in my current practices I am unlikely to place my communication of content expertise in a prominent position in the classroom. However, there are occasions (like in the anecdote about my resorting to lecturing in the graduate class) when I find my default position still traces itself back to what I have now learned is a dormant rather than a dead assumption; traces of my role from "Students Applaud Students" can still appear long after I had thought the assumption was revised.

And fourth, the assumptions present in your critical incidents will probably represent a mix of resonant and dissonant beliefs in relationship with your current work as a teacher. The work in the next chapter will help look at how these "roots" have a continuing influence on the "routes" we take in our teaching.

A colleague teaching in the undergraduate honors program was recently reflecting on his growth as a college teacher, and what we talked about stands as another example of the features of paradigmatic assumptions (as well as their relationship to causal and prescriptive assumptions). We were talking about the difficulty of uncovering and then acknowledging the deepest assumptions influencing our work. He told me the story that prompted him to examine his assumptions. In teaching a freshman class about the legends of King Arthur a number of years ago, he recalls spending the bulk of the semester explicating the history of British literature in preparation for having students explore the influence of Arthurian legends. He explained his experiences and touched on the expectations and values he brought to them; without prompting he talked about causal and prescriptive assumptions. He expected students would, by virtue of his approach, be prepared to see the relationships between the historical and the contemporary, and he expected them to be able to come to the same understandings he had. He valued, he said, his role as a scholar, disseminating the content in the way it had been disseminated to him.

A turning point came at the conclusion of the semester when he faced three realizations. He thought the class had gone particularly well from his perspective although he regretted not having much time to discuss the contemporary influence of the legends. And, he realized that he had, in fact, taught the course more as a prerequisite for the class, rather than the class he had intended to teach. Further, his review of student work made him realize that only a few select students "got it" (his words). He then recalled that he spent time blaming students' inattention, lack of preparation, and limited achievement for the results he saw. But at some later point, he began to reflect on his own role. He became curious about what had influenced his pedagogical choices when he developed and taught this course. As we talked about the nature of paradigmatic assumptions, he nodded in recognition of their deep-seatedness as well as in recognition that this was indeed the level of reflection he was trying to reach. The further he got into this search, he admitted, the greater the challenge: "When you try to put it into words, that's when you start questioning it." He echoed Maryellen Weimer's characterization in her book *Inspired College Teaching*: "Critical reflection does not ask easy questions. It hits hard on strongly held beliefs ..." (2010, p. 33). Given this, what can be done to help (using Ruth Brown's book title) *If at First You Do Not See* (1982)?

Note on Process

Trust the insights that you have gained at each step in the process of looking into your critical incidents as they provide you with constituent pieces of assumptions. You have the stories themselves, each selected through a process of considering the responses you recall they generated. Through revisiting your story-coding and the "because" sentences that expanded the details for what were identified as critical incidents, you will be grounded in the emotional power of each story. Doing so can also help balance the analysis and conceptualization that assumption-hunting invites.

After you identified a primary vantage point for each story, you used that to look at the roles played out within each. The roles of the teacher, student, and content, both within each story and across stories, gave you the opportunity to learn about patterns that repeat themselves in your educational history. Those insights may have helped you reflect on the influence those roles played in your changing conceptions of teaching and learning. Building as you have from incident to responses to roles—whether in notes, more extensive writing, or conversations—can enable you to gain the outlines of paradigmatic assumptions for individual incidents. You are thus engaged in the process of reviewing, in two different conceptions of that word: "reviewing" as in going back over, and "re-viewing" as in seeing in new ways. There is much to gain in addition to what you have already learned about the relationship between the history of your educational experiences and the directions your teaching has taken.

As a part of the process for seeking to articulate paradigmatic assumptions, you can also turn to the claims gathered in Chapter Five. The claims themselves were difficult to pull out of the stories, but doing so made visible some of the implicit and influential messages within them. Because the claims arise from stories identified as critical incidents, they can provide a bridge to paradigmatic assumptions. When the concept of "critical incident" was introduced in Chapter Three, it was characterized as most likely to be "flashpoints" (Woods, 1993, p. 1), "jolting events" (Eakin, 2008, p. 3), and, because of their prominent place in our memories, "highly charged moments and episodes that have enormous consequences for personal change and development" (Sikes, Measor, and Woods, 1985, p. 230). Through locating the shape of assumptions within the incidents' claims, roles, and responses, you will understand what makes the relationship among all of them visible. As a paradigmatic assumption in one incident comes to the surface, I am likely to begin to see those in other stories more easily. With the information gathered from looking at roles within and across incidents, and at claims and responses, components of these assumptions were given space to come to light in the process of critical reflection.

Persistence of Paradigmatic Assumptions

Because they are so fundamental as to be unconsciously influential to many aspects of our pedagogical choice making, Brookfield says that paradigmatic assumptions are not easily altered. They are, he says, open to change only after a series of contradictory evidence is visible (1985, p. 3). When Ronald walked into my classroom all of those mornings ago, I was not aware that his words and actions were setting up a series of incidents that would counter the paradigmatic assumptions which I had then held about the roles of teacher and learner. All that I knew was that his actions threw me off balance.

That September day, for each subsequent class period, I delivered my prepared (and well-rehearsed) script, distributed Warriner's grammar books, and then reseated students alphabetically. Each aspect of that first day announced in both words and actions that I should be in charge. Except for Ronald, students' actions reinforced my beliefs (my paradigmatic assumptions) about how things should be. I remember no other counter script that day, but as the year progressed there were some. My first year of teaching was a liminal space where many insights were possible if I had only paid them more deliberate attention.

There is an energy that can result from making a careful examination of teaching, as has been illustrated earlier with examples from professional journals; the very process of reflecting on classroom experiences can become a story itself. Neurobiologist K. D. Tanner gave herself the same assignment that she gives students at the conclusion of an introductory biology class: Write a 1200–1500 word essay responding to these questions: "'What have you learned in this class that will continue to influence you for years to come?

How have you learned these things?"" (2011, p. 114). As a result of her own reflection she published an essay, "Moving Theory into Practice: A Reflection on Teaching a Large Introductory Biology Course for Majors." The context of her story, a 300-student class, was a new experience for her. This had an impact on the assumptions she recognized in her work, her use of certain teaching practices, and her simultaneous reflections of her teaching and student learning. She chronicles "worries and concerns in preparing to teach the course for the first time" (p. 113) and finds that the experience ultimately led her to reflect on being "struck by several insights that I would like to share" (p. 114).

In recounting insights gained from what she found through her own reflections and what she gleaned from students' reflections, she writes that there are insights "that I believe will continue to inform me for years to come" (p. 113). Throughout her essay there are expectations (causal assumptions) and values (prescriptive assumptions). Some of the beliefs she implies that she held before the experience were contradicted. Tanner's conviction that her practices had been altered by her experience is a story filled with energy for teaching and for professional growth. Without an opportunity to consider the roots of her practices in the critical incidents of her educational biography, it is difficult to link her reflections to the most deeply held paradigmatic assumptions. As you seek these deepest of levels in your own reflections, the energy for understanding your teaching and for strengthening your practice have an even greater potential for transformation.

As I look at my own collection of critical incidents, I find that most of them did counter the resistant-to-change paradigmatic assumptions by which I was unconsciously guided at the time. Over a period of years, my stories "Shoulder-Shrugger," "Students Applaud Students," and "Students Asked Me to Leave" turned out to be a collection of pivotal incidents (although I did not recognize them as such at the time). Each of the incidents repeated Ronald's challenge to my causal, prescriptive, and paradigmatic assumptions and set up an eventual shift in my teaching practices. Since then, I have grown and changed in my teaching, but with this work on assumptions I have come to see some are still present, deeply buried, in my work.

In Chapter Eight, the ways that such past assumptions still can unexpectedly show themselves in teaching will be thought through. I am drawn to novelist Sandra Cisneros's idea expressed in *The House on Mango Street*: "You can never have too much sky" (1984, p. 39). My commitment to strengthening my teaching grows in proportion to my understanding of it; as the scope of what I see broadens, the possibilities multiply.

Next Steps

As you conclude this chapter, you have stories which began with a few details and descriptive titles and which have now become doorways through which you have gained entrance to a fuller view of their place in your teaching and learning. In *Living Autobiographically: How We Create Identity in Narrative*, Eakin's belief is that "our life stories are not merely *about* us but in an inescapable and profound way *are* us" (2008, p. x, italics in original). Walking through our stories in critical reflection is more a process than a destination, but through the process, we can grow into new and productive understandings about the enterprise of teaching. In the origins of the stories, and our current interpretation and analysis of them, contexts walk with us.

Borton (1970) has a reflective framework that Rolfe, Jasper, and Freshwater (2011) cite as being a helpful heuristic when approaching reflection. The questions in the framework may be useful to you as yet another way to excavate assumptions. Each question in the heuristic points to a different stance in the process. Asking "What?" "So what?" and "Now what?" moves through observing to theorizing to acting based on the influence of the responses (p. 42). In "Students Asked Me to Leave" the "What?" relates to the fact that

I intended (that is, expected) that if I lectured to students on what I perceived they needed, they would learn. In that story asking myself "So what?" leads me to articulate a value: I valued my role of content expert as the primary way students would learn material. And when I further ask myself "Now what?" I find that through the other two assumptions, I can now see that I believed the role of the teacher was to demonstrate content expertise that would, in and of itself, lead to student learning. Years of experiences have led me to revise these assumptions, but the paradigmatic one still has some, albeit minimal, presence in my work.

In all of my critical incidents, my interpretation of them is context-dependent. The prototypical view of teacher and teaching that I had in my head on the first day of teaching in "First Day" was influenced by contexts. These contexts included in part how I "played school" as a young girl, how I internalized my earliest expectations of responsibility as an oldest child, how I experienced college life as a first-generation college student, and how I accepted the preponderance of "Miss Grundy" and "Mr. Gradgrind" as my role models. These contexts and others provided me with views on the presence and use of power. The "First Day" story was further influenced by the features of the school in which it took place, models from my own education through college, my inexperience and naïveté, and the fact that I was among the first female teachers in the school other than the teachers for girls' physical education and home economics. These are some of the contextual factors that contributed to what I thought, expected, felt, and did at the time. They also contributed to leaving such a deeply rooted impression on me that this Walker, Minnesota, classroom has persisted in my memories while my classroom experiences have marched on. The contextual factors in which the critical incidents sit as we tell about the "self then" and as we move to "the self thinking about future selves" (Bruner, 1990, p. 121) have been in the background.

Chapter Eight will consider questions about the contexts that have influenced the "what" of the identification of critical incidents and the "so what" of the analysis. In further pursuing the "now what," the concluding chapter will look at how the reappearances of long-held paradigmatic assumptions may influence our work even years after we think we have left them behind. And the book will conclude by looking at the implications of insights gained through each stage of this process for professional growth. Stories we lived, stories we tell, and the stories we build can simultaneously challenge and reward us. Brazilian educator Paulo Freire's words invite us to continue looking at the influence of our stories: "That you give yourself to it critically and with ever-expanding curiosity" (1998, p. 27).

8

Storied Teaching

At a personal level, narratives are important to us not
only because they tell us about our past lives but
because they enable us to make sense of the present.
                                                    (Watson, 2009, p. 470)

A colleague who is a professor in a department of criminology
and criminal justice opens her freshman course on international human rights by passing a number of kaleidoscopes around
the room. She asks students to consider the images they see through
the cylinder as different perspectives related to the focus of the
course. Although most students have previously looked through a
kaleidoscope, using it as a metaphor is new to them. She enables
them to consider how the bits and pieces of objects seen within a
circle of mirrors are like the contextual details that influence the
perspective the viewer holds up to his or her eye. When the objects
reflect off those mirrors as the viewer looks through one end and
light enters the other, the perspectives change as the students turn
the cylinder. With each turning, new details emerge and what one
sees shifts to take into account the new information. Multiple views
and multiple viewings yield an increasing amount of information,
and expand the perspectives one can grasp.

I have used a number of metaphors at each stage in this book to
build a view of the work because the process of working to see what

our stories teach us is difficult to put into words. This kaleidoscope metaphor that my colleague uses captures the spirit of this concluding chapter because multiple personal perspectives continue to be available to arrange in an endless variety of patterns, even as the book itself ends. The fragments of story details combine with each other and reflect each other's features when the narratives are turned in unexpected ways. Perspectives shift and new relationships come into view between and among stories, past and present.

The final chapter in a book is most often written to tie a subject together and to conclude the discussion. In this book, however, such a conclusion is antithetical. The goal of the book is not to lead to a single picture of one's assumptions about teaching with a corresponding singular vision of the implications. The work is far more complex and is instead meant to open up a myriad of personalized insights along the way. The three major stages in the book are comprised of different twists of the kaleidoscope, each providing ways to let in light so the images from the stories reflect off the mirrors, and an unending series of insights result.

In a brief review of the process, this chapter will first draw on one critical incident in my repertoire, "Students Applaud Students," to illustrate the individual and cumulative surprises that accompany each stage. Each turn in the process gave me additional insights into the underpinnings of my teaching, and in my tracing these you may see the interrelationships that continue to unfold in your stories more clearly. The chapter then moves to probing the contexts of stories. Although contexts have been referred to within each stage, they can now be viewed as foundational influences that are infused throughout. The discussion of contexts leads back to assumptions. When contexts are over-laid on assumptions and critical incidents, some broad and powerful understandings can fill in the patterns that have emerged throughout our work in this book.

One way to link insights from this process with current practices so implications for growth become visible is to add a look at tensions (moments of discomfort or disruption) present in one's teaching.

Some tensions are noticeable, others lie underneath those that are more easily recognized. Like the work on contexts, work on tensions draws on all of the insights we have gained and stops the turning of the kaleidoscope so we can see what comes into sharper focus. Becoming cognizant of "sticking points" in our current teaching can lead to identifying some foundations of those tensions and then to linking them to understanding and growth. This aspect of the work opens up potential incongruities between teaching actions and assumptions. Because of this, here is the point in this work where I find myself most vulnerable. Within the kaleidoscopic colors of the cumulative details and insights, I now start to recognize some new relationships that begin to form contrasting patterns I did not expect and would have been unprepared to recognize if I had had hints of their presence earlier. Because it is within the vulnerability that the potential for deepening understanding and growth can emerge, the book concludes by taking stock of what pictures are present and what lies ahead as we lean into growth.

Every time I walk through this process, I am reminded of the challenges it presents, its rigors, its surprises, and even its frustrations. As I return to the work because it carries a promise of more insights, I am rewarded by moments of clarity about my stories and about how they might assist me (as Watson points out in the opening chapter quote) in "mak[ing] sense of the present." More light enters the kaleidoscope.

Growing through the Process

Here is how one of my critical incidents grew more vivid as it caught the reflection of additional details through the process. I was surprised that "Students Applaud Students" came to mind so quickly in Chapter Two when I originally put together my repertoire of stories. Why did this come to the surface of my memory? When I applied the codings in Chapter Three, I was again surprised, this time by the intensity of my responses to the incident. Continuing the work in that chapter, I added the "because" statements after each code, and this gave me insights into how stories, particularly like "Students Applaud Students," and "First Day" (with Ronald), may in fact be related to each other. These two stories happened years apart, but the codings and "because" statements showed they were unexpectedly resonant.

When I began to pick apart the roles played by teacher, student, and content (Chapter Four), the patterns I saw started to teach me about some of the undercurrents in my teaching biography. At the conclusion of that chapter where I worked across more than a single story to synthesize the roles present, I had a sense of a gathering of insights about influences on my teaching practices. How do those impact my work beyond my seeking to replicate some practices and counter others as I grow in the role of teacher?

At that juncture, I found myself sitting back with the "Students Applaud Students" story notes that I had been keeping, now adding more details to my view. When it came next to identifying claims in each of my stories, the process sometimes felt like I was trying to channel someone else's psyche. But, I kept going back to some of my earlier insights—I am the one who remembered the story after all these years, and it is unlikely to have been an equally memorable one for anyone else. So, I dug deeper into the story that by then had become far more than an interesting anecdote. How I continue to come to understand "Students Applaud Students" is influenced by other stories and stages of analysis, and it in turn contributes to them. No matter how you have walked through this process, at this point you are likely to have had moments of surprise, moments of wonder, moments of contemplation, and moments of discomfort. Telling one or more stories or talking with someone about what has come to you as insights can help balance the findings and unsettlings that you may have come to recognize.

The work on claims led to the ways in which assumptions can become visible in the metaphorical kaleidoscope. As I worked to deliberately identify expectations, values, and then beliefs for critical incidents, the additional insights—even for the causal and prescriptive assumptions—felt alien. As I began to recognize myself in those rotating mirrors, I also began to recognize the presence of the students who applauded their colleagues, of Ronald, of the shoulder-shrugger, of Freire, and others from what had become my "critical incidents." In this, I became increasingly aware of the impact of contexts on how my perspectives were shaped. In the same way that the students who enroll in my colleague's human rights course come to recognize the impact of contexts on the images they saw through the kaleidoscope, I recognized it too.

Contexts

Without considering the contexts that accompany critical incidents and their assumptions, insights gained through reflection are incomplete. "Students Applaud Students" took place in a context, in which, for instance, I had first modeled teaching when I "taught school" to my siblings in a "Winter Saturday Classroom," the story that opens this book. In both stories, as well as in "First Day," I was relatively new to teaching, I was not certain of the content, and I actually hoped students would not ask questions because I found my shaky expertise would become visible. Each of our stories has a backstory, a set of dimensions that makes a particular moment in time the one that gets stuck in our memory banks.

If you are talking with a colleague or family member as you do this work on stories, maybe you found yourself filling in information about the circumstances that brought about the incident. These details augment the plot line that has been your primary focus. Paying attention to contexts can further illuminate the origins of assumptions that contribute to understanding how they can come to be confirmed, countered, or revised in our teaching. In order to trace the consequences of having uncovered some assumptions, this chapter pays deliberate attention to the nature of contexts—those features of background, time, place, and circumstance—that elevate a routine moment to a significant one embedded in memory. A seemingly insignificant incident that happened to me not long ago illustrates the interrelationship between past contexts and current incidents. As you follow this interrelationship, it may prompt you to bring in details about the contexts that played a role in your own critical incidents and thus, in the formation of assumptions that are present in aspects of your work today.

Example of Layered Influences of Contexts

A recent routine event surprisingly led me to reflect on a past story, then to that story's contexts, and then further to an understanding of one of my related teaching practices. The incident involved my getting a manuscript returned with reviewer comments. Three supportive words at the end of the page, "Proceed with Confidence," eventually sent me back to another trio of words that a very different kind of reviewer used to respond to my writing years ago. It is the context of that distant critical incident that enables me to place the current event into a perspective and leads to an understanding of a related assumption and its visibility in one of my teaching practices. The contextual information places the initial critical incident in a deeply personal context that then reveals some assumptions I did not realize that I both carry and work to confirm through my teaching practices.

Mr. Berg's Comment

Laboring in the world's largest open-pit iron ore mine and supporting a wife and five children, my father saw the regular delivery of milk bottles as a sign of pride and prosperity for my parents. With little extra money and no experiences with higher education, he didn't have the option to foster college aspirations for an eldest daughter. Since marriage and children would be sure to follow, such extended schooling would not be a wise investment of whatever meager funds might be squeezed out of the food and milk budget. When, however, a tenth-grade English teacher assigned a research paper, I thought role-playing was in order. I would pretend this was a college assignment and would tackle it with a fervor and intellect that would please the teacher I idealized as a model of intellect.

I looked up "research" in the card catalogue of the public library and found the then-current edition of *Form and Style in Theses* by Campbell (1954). I checked out this early edition spiral-bound guide and set out to research my topic, "Alternatives to Traditional Schooling." Campbell guided me through a statement of the problem, a review of the literature, an explanation of the findings, and the place of the findings in the literature. So much more rested on Mr. Berg's response to the paper than he could have ever imagined. When he eventually returned our papers, mine had a three-word comment written in a crimson flourish next to Statement of Problem: "More than necessary." The three words were written in calligraphy worthy of being framed. "More than necessary." My heart sank and, given the context my aspirations brought to this effort, I read his words as a judgment of my dreams—they were, he seemed to be saying, "More than necessary."

The manuscript reviewer would have had no idea that the historical context of my story about Mr. Berg would accompany my reading of the review. Following a series of responses and recommendations, the reviewer included a lengthy summary comment, and the entire review concluded, "Proceed with Confidence." I responded emotionally before I responded intellectually to the comment, and I carried the three words around in my head like an unexpected gift. It did not become clear to me until days later, after I had posted the words on the board above my computer, that these words were related to the ones from the earlier incident, that this recent three-word pair presented a stark contrast with the earlier ones.

When I have told this "Mr. Berg's Comment" story before (Shadiow, 2007), I have been aware that it left a legacy influencing my beliefs about teaching. Gunn would point to my story as an illustration of her point that "the autobiographical self comes *from* somewhere" (1982, p. 15, italics in the original). In fact, in reading professional literature on teaching, I have always been drawn to the material on writing effective comments on student papers. When I sit with a stack of exams or essays I am guided by a synthesis of what I have read over the years: use a student's name, tie recommendations to their effects on the reader, and point out a goal for improving the next piece of work. I do not know if I have ever tied the "Mr. Berg's Comment" to how to respond to student work until now. But clearly Mr. Berg is present and I continue to chafe against his example. Crites (1971) draws the line from my Mr. Berg incident to the current contrasting one involving the reviewer: "Experience is illuminated only by the subtle process of reflection" (p. 300). The result of my understanding of the timeline that stretches between these two incidents is an insight into my assumptions about the teacher-student relationship.

I include this story because it illustrates the role that contexts play in the powerful shaping of assumptions. Contexts elevated the moment I looked at Mr. Berg's comment to a critical incident that would stay with me. Critical incidents are stories intertwined with the emotions that led them to that designation with the codings in Chapter Three, and those emotions are inextricably linked to places, times, people, and sociocultural features. You may or may not have sensed this as you have worked through the process; here is a moment to pay deliberate attention to contexts.

Select one or two critical incidents and give some thought to the contexts that surrounded them at the time they happened. Jot down a few notes, talk with someone, or just think about the details surrounding the initial story. What gave the plot line personal meaning to you when it might not have had the same impact on someone else? Consider the extent to which different critical incidents have similar contextual features. "Students Applaud Students" and "First Day," for instance, both have fear-of-not-knowing aspects in the contexts, and both occurred at the beginning of my relationships with students, where I was seeking to assert my "teacher self."

When I try to trace the assumptions for the Mr. Berg critical incident, I envision him as the primary actor, but I am unable to pull out the roles or assumptions inherent in his work except for how they affected me. I am so emotionally connected to the story even now that I can only work through the assumptions from my own point of view, my "self now recalling my self then" (Bruner, 1990, p. 121). As I scrutinize my retelling, I find my basic action was to turn in an assignment and wait eagerly (even impatiently) for his response. In doing this,

I *expected* an affirmation of the way I had accomplished the work (a causal assumption);

I expected this affirmation because I *valued* the role an effective teacher had in the recognition of student potential (a prescriptive assumption); and

I valued that role because I *believed* supportive recognition by a teacher was a key to learning (a paradigmatic assumption).

This set of assumptions, as difficult as they can be to articulate, may seem like common sense, but one of the characteristics of assumptions is that when articulated they "make the knowing explicit" (Schön, 1987, p. 25).

One of the teaching strategies I have used over the years rests in large part on the paradigmatic assumption rooted in the Mr. Berg story. In order to be responsive to students in a class, I have come to use—mostly unconsciously—the strategy of identifying a small group of students whose reactions to class I trust and use as bell-wethers during a course; I glance regularly at these students in class and I use their reactions to what is happening in class to influence my subsequent actions. If these key students look quizzical, I pause to give another example; if they look engaged, I move on; if they look distracted, I shift the pace of what we are doing. I have even gone so far as to tell new faculty that this is one of the ways to personalize a class and recognize student input. It now occurs to me that this little technique is part of a constellation of practices I pride myself on doing. They are not just things I do, but they are a part of how I define myself as a teacher.

In working on assumptions I can see that the reason I actually obsess about a collection of like practices is because they are tied to that underlying paradigmatic assumption: supportive recognition by a teacher is a key to learning. This is one of the aspects of teaching that is in my teaching DNA, a part of my personal "signature pedagogy." So much so that it is habit, a tacit understanding that this is who I am as I teach. Not too many years ago I was faced with evidence that "the sincerity of their [teachers'] intentions does not guarantee the purity of their practice" (Brookfield, 1995, p. 1). This critical incident, "Perception of Credibility," brought me abruptly to the intersection of the intentions and actions related to the teaching practice I so unquestionably employed as a counterpoint to Mr. Berg.

Perception of Credibility

I learned the term *perception of credibility* at a conference session discussion on how undergraduates judged the worth of different sources, particularly on the Internet. For example, do students perceive Wikipedia as a credible source? I went away from the session intrigued by the concept of perception of credibility and marked a note in my conference program wondering if the concept could be applied to people as sources, too. Months later, when I was filing the conference materials, I ran across my note. I can't exactly recall how I found my way to making this link, but I connected the concept *perception of credibility* with my practice of perceiving a small group of students in a class as being credible reviewers of the teaching and learning. I wondered if there were any kind of pattern in my recognition of those students, and I decided to select one course and do a little informal study to see what I might learn. Frankly, I expected to find a confirmation of my practice as an equalitarian one. I did not.

I took a series of small steps to answer the question, "In my class, who do I perceive as being credible enough to use their reactions to class as a guide to the teaching?" I took two primary steps—I looked at the class roster to see whose names and faces came immediately to mind, and I observed my own teaching (the "view from the balcony") and took conscious note of the students I looked to during a week of class. I put all of the names together and then examined the list to see what I might find there.

I found that the students I selected as my bellwether of responses to the class were students the most like me: female, middle-class, eager to learn, engaged in the content, intellectually curious, and white. I was stunned. I tried the analysis in another class and came up with the same result. Then I looked at students I sanctioned, those who stuck out to me as outliers—inattentive, distracting, disengaged—and I did a quick analysis of who they were and what characteristics they had. These were students to whom I sent nonverbal messages. I too often took their reactions as evidence that my imposter fears had merit. Strangely, my analysis showed that these students were also like me, but the me who would underachieve when I found college classes boring or irrelevant. More significantly, I started to get a sense that both of these findings only foreshadowed what I sensed was a part of my teaching that would be even more difficult to face. I hesitantly decided to look at students whose names I did not yet know, students who were a part of the class but students I just "let be" in the class. What I feared might be true was proved. They were the students most unlike me. Many were older-than-average, students

of color, nonnative speakers of English, and many were male. I was
appalled.

In my little study (more fully explored in "Classroom Interactions: Constructing a Room with a View," Shadiow, April-June
2010), I found that my practice stood in direct contradiction to how
I thought about my work. Given the contexts of the class, my professional experiences, and my assumptions about what contributed
to student learning, I saw myself as a teacher acting on my commitment to equity.

It's not that the practice of being guided by student responses
is a bad or ineffective one. Research says otherwise. But my intentions about recognizing students and how I unquestioningly implemented them were contradictory. The link from teaching practice
to intention traces back to an assumption that grew out of my perception of the critical incident, "Mr. Berg's Comment." My resulting conviction was that I would work diligently to place recognition
of students in a central place in my teaching principles.

Seeing Contextual Interplay

A number of professors have contributed their own stories to the
professional literature, writing about the interplay between contexts, assumptions, and growth. What follows are brief glimpses of
how three different faculty members turned the reflectively kaleidoscopic process of critical reflection to their own work. These professional and highly personal stories illustrate the presence of four features: initial events (that is, critical incidents), the impact of contexts, the role of tensions (that is, "expectations that went awry"),
and the consideration of assumptions. I include these three brief
examples here to help you see the features as they reflect off of each
other.

Sociology professor Kent Sandstrom writes about what he
learned as he looked closely at his teaching in his essay "Embracing

Modest Hopes: Lessons from the Beginning of a Teaching Journey" (1999). He turns his analytic eye first toward the assumptions he initially brought to his teaching and to the undergraduate course, "Sociology of Everyday Life." Then, in order to understand his experiences there, he broadened the scope of his attention to consider the contexts that as a sociologist he understood as having an impact on teaching and learning: "the inter-related contexts—cultural, regional, institutional, and departmental" (p. 520). Faculty, he concludes, make "the mistake of downplaying the significance of the context of teaching" (p. 525). Near the end of the essay he has a section on "Learning About Oneself as a Teacher" (pp. 524–527). As he explores assumptions he initially brought to his work he acknowledges the tensions that resulted from them. When he concludes that the understanding of contexts can play a role in addressing those tensions, his own detailed essay stands as an illustration of his point.

In "'Critically Reflective Pedagogy': Teaching Sociology after Hurricanes Katrina and Rita," sociology professor Stan Weeber (2011) describes the process he went through to "open a window to the thought processes that accompanied the substantial pedagogic leap" (p. 2) he took as a consequence of the reopening of his university after a thirty-seven-day closure following the hurricanes. This was a time when he admits that the level of scrutiny he brought to this work "left me struggling with competing narratives" (p. 5). The contexts that usually influenced his work were beyond disrupted, they were chaotic. The students, the faculty, the department, the institution, and the region all were faced with reentry, and the stories were all in need of being rewritten, given the wrenching uncertainty he describes.

At the intersection of his own educational biography, his past experiences with the four sociology classes he was teaching, and the dramatic and pervasive impact of the hurricanes, he felt like "the director of a play for which there was no script" (p. 5). Stephen Brookfield's work on critically reflective teaching was profoundly influential for Weeber as he worked with students to build new classroom environments marked by the "democratic reconstruction" of the course and by "mutual respect and collaborativeness" (p. 5). Throughout the essay and particularly in the subsections "Examining Our Own Biographies" and "Student and Teacher Outcomes," Weeber carefully explicates the intertwined threads of the personal, contextual, and the pedagogical. The changes in his courses and the changes in his pedagogy reverberated as he became aware of assumptions, preoccupations, and obsessions that collectively had "lulled me into a false sense of security" (p. 8).

Coming from the context of the social work profession, Helen Hickson (2011) writes about uncovering and addressing her assumptions as she learns to "reflect, explore, and learn" (p. 829). In "Critical Reflection: Reflecting on Learning to be Reflective," she speaks to the nested process of looking into tensions—instances where she experienced puzzlement, confusion, even irritation in her work. She worked to become conscious of how and why such analysis contributes to her professional development. For Hickson, moving into scrutiny of contexts ("experience, values, and gender influences" (p. 836) meant the discovery that "the deconstruction of language and meaning can assist with exploring and unsettling assumptions" (p. 833). When she set a goal of approaching familiar situations in unfamiliar ways as a result of analyzing underlying principles, she concludes, "I found that, over time, I became more confident and open to examining assumptions" (p. 838).

She describes her process as unearthing three specific areas of tensions—points that generate unease when her underlying assumptions were countered: "control, uncertainty, and change" (p. 838). In those instances, she used a key question to explore the tensions she found: "'But why does this [the unsettling event] matter?'" (p. 836). Through the process she, like Sandstrom and Weeber, moves to reevaluate and revise assumptions that undergirded classroom practices. One example from Hickson's work illustrates this shift. Initially she says an assumption about control was that "If no one is in control, it can be dangerous or threatening" (p. 834). After working to understand the contexts in which this arose and the contexts in which it had impact, she describes it evolved to "When I am not in control, it does not mean the situation is out of control" (p. 825).

These three stories of heightened and substantial scrutiny of pedagogical work show that there is not necessarily a linear progression to awareness and reexamination of assumptions. However, the essays do all have at least four features in common: (1) explication of a critical incident, (2) consideration of the impact of contexts, (3) scrutiny of the different levels of assumptions, and (4) recognition of the presence of tensions. These features can be seen as shapes bordering the colors of related details in your personal kaleidoscope. The shape of contexts in my "Mr. Berg's Comment," for instance, frames details about familial expectations and sociocultural constructs. Similarly each of the other three features outlines details from explorations of your stories. "Putting ideas into a circle or wheel," writes Wilson in *Research Is Ceremony* (2008), "indicates that they are interrelated. . .that ideas flow from one to the next in a cyclical fashion. A change in one affects the others. . ." (p. 70).

Consider the first three of the above features—critical incidents, contexts, and assumptions. Starting with any of those elements that you feel will be a productive door to the others, note details that fill out that concept. In "Mr. Berg's Comment," for example, I use *context* to access the incident. From there, I move to another feature and think about how it is intertwined with the first. Again in "Mr. Berg's Comment," the second feature (critical incident) flows from context and then back again. When you have begun to see some of the relationships, add the third feature and again look through the details into the intersections. In "Mr. Berg's Comment," the assumptions (the third feature) build from and into the others. Picturing this as a Venn diagram with overlapping borders, you are working toward looking into those overlapping sections. If you are seeking precision, you will be frustrated; if you trust your process and give it space to happen, you will be more likely to bring those interrelationships to the foreground. Because you are working with your stories in a way that resonates for you, there is no replicable, lock-step process here. Instead of spending time seeking one, tune into how you sense that the features inform a deeper understanding of each other. Persist with patience.

However you chose to do that step—thought, conversation, notes or narrative, sketch, or diagram—you have gotten closer to the marrow of what your stories have to tell. With the additional feature of "tensions," the link between the work so far and professional growth will be drawn.

Tensions

Since being introduced in Chapter Six, the concept of tensions as related to one's teaching has been characterized as unsettling moments when instability, disruption, or discomfort has come to the fore. They are not necessarily paralyzing moments; they may be merely responses to an annoying situation. The goal, as Stenberg (2005) writes, is to recognize the potential of such tensions: "Moments of perplexity, disorientation, even chaos—can lead, upon reflection and inquiry, to new pedagogical possibilities" (p. 66).

Chapter Seven opened with a short vignette where I felt rushed by having too much material to cover in too little time near the end of a class period, so I resorted to the equivalent of speed-lecturing. Minutes before class concluded, I realized my very actions were contradicting what, in fact, I was lecturing about. Because this moment stood in such stark contrast to my intentions, I could not "let it go" and chalk it up to an ineffective response to time pressure. With some other similar moments I do just note them and move on. Others, like this one, remind me that, in teaching, one of my "default modes" is to lecture. When John Dewey wrote about the nature of reflection in his 1910 book *How We Think*, he said that one of the elements leading to critical reflection was "a state of perplexity, hesitation, doubt" (p. 9), and that in the situations "where the shoe pinches, analytic examination is indicated" (p. 216). In those moments, I find little immediate relief knowing that he also wrote, "Reflective thinking is more or less troublesome because it involves overcoming the inertia that inclines one to accept suggestions at face value; it involves willingness to endure a condition of mental unrest and disturbance" (p. 13). Looking *into* some tensions in our teaching, moments when the "shoe pinches," rather than overlooking them can contribute to uncovering avenues for growth. Adding knowledge of any patterns of tensions to the critical incidents, contexts, and assumptions can open relational insights.

> Give some thought to the types of instances in your teaching where you experience either brief or enduring times of disequilibrium. Some faculty talk about having "hot buttons" that are perpetual annoyances, others make comments that begin with, "I don't know why I did this but. . .". The tensions may evolve from changing contexts, from challenges, or from times when, as Weeber writes, we are like a "director of a play for which there is no script" (2011, p. 5). Jot down some of those moments in order to see if there are any patterns to them. You may want to ask, as Hickson does, "Why does this [unsettling event] matter?" (2011, p. 833).

When Hickson undertook the close look at tension spots in her teaching she identified three patterns in those tensions—they were, she observes, about control, uncertainty, and change (2011, p. 828). Considering all of the critical incidents I have told and scrutinized in this book, I would also identify three themes in the tensions that most unsettle me: power, control, and expertise. These themes are underneath small discomforts like my being asked questions for which I do not know the answers and failing to remember student names when I meet students outside of class; they are visible to me when I am faced with a switch in teaching assignments and when I try to moderate a contentious class discussion; they are evident to me in my reluctance to increasingly use more technology in class and when I put end-of-semester student course evaluations aside rather than read them the day I receive them. These six instances may be examples that for others do not reach the threshold of Dewey's pinching shoe where "analytic examination is indicated" (1910, p. 216), but the contexts of my stories and assumptions make them so for me.

> If you have not yet done so, note some of the moments when you are thrown off balance during daily routines. If you have done this already, have you thought of more to add? Whether you have listed three or ten, fewer or more, look closely to see if there are any patterns there, any themes they appear to have in common. Because of all of the work you have done beginning with identifying a repertoire of stories, there may be some themes that become readily apparent, themes that "fit" with how you experience the role of teacher, learner, or content. These themes can open up opportunities for pursuing professional growth, so I suggest you might even put this work aside for a while and take this way of considering tensions with you as food for thought until you are ready to return.

In Chapter Seven, I referred to an essay by Searby and Tripses (2011) to illustrate that closely examining one's pedagogy demands "going to the balcony." This process of reflecting on teaching encompasses insights gained regarding the broad brushstroke views of roles, but then it also includes paying attention to moments, moments when we can step outside of ourselves to make an observation that can become a site for growth. To move from becoming aware of tensions, to opening up those tensions to learn where they might spring from and why, to considering origins and impact brings us back to critical incidents. I stood on this proverbial balcony in "Perception of Credibility" when I scrutinized a routine practice.

After doing so, I came to understand the impact of that tension between my intents and actions by uncovering the links between the incident, "Mr. Berg's Comments," and the assumptions it gave rise to. Then, I left the "balcony" to pursue ways my new understandings could guide me in developing as a teacher. Given a life spent reading and writing, my instincts often send me to books—in this case, I reread Charles Taylor's book, *Multiculturalism and the Politics of Recognition* (1992). Here, I decided, was something I owed to my students to work on. But, I also talked with a trusted colleague, reconsidered some of my teaching practices, and looked beyond my well-meaning intentions to what they enabled and constrained for students. A brief family anecdote shared by essayist Scott Russell Sanders at the beginning of his collection of essays, *Staying Put: Making a Home in a Restless World* (1993), describes this process. When the Sanders family would move to a new home during his years of growing up, he observed his father always going into the yard, picking up a piece of dirt, and putting it on his tongue. One day, young Scott asked him what he was doing. His father explained, "'Just trying to figure out where I am'" (p. xiii). Moving from tensions through three layers of assumptions each informed by critical incidents invites me to "figure out where I am."

Leaning into Growth

The goal of becoming deeply conscious of tensions and deeply aware of their origins is to find ways to grow in our teaching. The learning that results from an examination of assumptions, Mezirow writes (1990), can lead to the "making of new or revised interpretation of meaning of an experience, which guides subsequent understanding, appreciation, and action" (p. 1). Assumptions that I work to affirm through my teaching have been shaped by experiences, research, and professional development, among other means. When tensions do arise, I am able to gain new perspectives on them through coming to understand what assumptions I am struggling to counter and which ones serve me well. Both can guide me to heightened appreciation of the web of intents and actions I can understand and grow with.

Faculty developer Barbara Millis writes an essay chronicling "my own evolving journey in the classroom" (2009, p. 17). In this, her growth coalesces around a specific approach to teaching that opened up some assumptions she held about the nature of learning and the roles she and students brought to that learning. "Becoming an Effective Teacher Using Cooperative Learning: A Personal Odyssey" takes her from the claims her past experiences led her to make about what is desirable in teaching to a paradigm-shifting workshop she attended in the 1980s. Throughout her essay she demonstrates that growth in one's teaching can be spurred in any number of ways, but that deliberate attention to what our stories tell us can help us lean into that development. "Caring teachers grow over time, aided by self-reflection, reading, workshops, peer mentors. . ." (p. 20). There are many avenues for achieving ongoing development in our profession, and many points that present us with opportunities to begin.

Some incidents we identify as critical today will go away tomorrow, and new ones of profound influence will appear although they may not be recognized as such until years later. Who would have thought that my anecdote about teaching school on a wintery afternoon in Northern Minnesota would open a book about reflection on teaching? Would I have identified the "Students Ask Me to Leave" or "First Day" stories as critical incidents the day, week, or month they happened? Although I was conscious at the time that my experience with Paulo Freire was a significant one, I do not think I recognized it as a moment of profound influence in my work on critical reflection. It seems appropriate in these concluding pages to draw on Freire's words about the power of all this professional curiosity that is behind the search of ways to lean into growth: "The more we practice methodically our capacity to question, to compare, to doubt, and to weigh, the more efficaciously curious we become" (1998, p. 61). That brings us back to the kaleidoscope metaphor that opened this chapter.

Next Steps

I used to collect different kinds of kaleidoscopes because to me they offered mystery and rewards. One of my favorites—one that illustrates what my colleague was using to demonstrate about gleaning multiple perspectives—fits here in talking about next steps in this process. With this kaleidoscope the end opposite the eyepiece actually snaps off. This allows the viewer to add very personal objects to that end of the cylinder so those objects are the ones that form patterns and which reflect each other in the multiple mirrors. Looking through the scope then presents a series of surprises about how the different bits and pieces relate to each other when the kaleidoscope sleeve is turned. There is no expectation that the patterns will remain static. Recognizing the absence of certainty is as key to this process as it is in the beginning of Dorothy Allison's *Two or Three Things I Know for Sure* (1995). Aunt Dot responds to her niece who observes that her aunt seems to know everything: "[T]here's only two or three things I know for sure. . . Only two or three things. . . Of course it's never the same things, and I'm never as sure as I'd like to be" (p. 5). This is to say that the next steps in the process of critical reflection involve a willingness to play.

Maybe surprisingly to you, the word "play" appears in this concluding section. It is time to take another walk, to recognize that with the serious work of excavating assumptions, play has a part. Over a century ago Dewey's discussion of reflective thinking included this promise: "To give the mind free play is not to encourage toying with a subject, but is to be interested in the unfolding of the subject on its own account" (1910, p. 219). I take the "unfolding of the subject" as a reference to each of us, to our teacher-selves as we interact with students, learning, content, and contexts. The three stages laid out in this book are entry points for the kind of play to which Dewey refers. Use the work to find out which people in your stories accompany you along the way. Who are the students who still live within your teaching practices? Where have traces of your current teaching practices appeared before in your critical incidents? What do the tensions you experience in teaching suggest it would be fruitful to explore? What will unfold when you take your assumptions into account? Are you ready to play?

References

Adams, D. *The Hitchhiker's Guide to the Galaxy.* New York: Pocket Books, 1979.

Allende, I. *Eva Luna.* Tr. Margaret Sayers Peden. New York: Bantam, 1989.

Allison, D. *Two or Three Things I Know for Sure.* New York: Plume, 1995.

Angelo, T. A., and Cross, K. P. *College Assessment Techniques: A Handbook for College Teachers.* 2nd ed. San Francisco: Jossey-Bass, 1993.

Argyris, C., and Schön, D. *Theory in Practice. Increasing Professional Effectiveness.* San Francisco: Jossey-Bass, 1974.

Bain, K. *What the Best College Teachers Do.* Cambridge: Harvard University Press, 2004.

Banks, R. *Cloudsplitter.* New York: HarperCollins, 1998.

Barkley, E. F. *Student Engagement Techniques: A Handbook for College Faculty.* San Francisco: Jossey-Bass, 2010.

Barkley, E. F., Cross, K. P., and Major, C. H. *Collaborative Learning Techniques: A Handbook for College Faculty.* San Francisco: Jossey-Bass, 2005.

Barr, R. B., and Tagg, J. "From Teaching to Learning: A New Paradigm for Undergraduate Education." *Change,* 1995, *27*(6), 12–25.

Berry, W. *What Are People For?* New York: North Point Press, 1990.

Boyer, E. L. *Ernest Boyer: Selected Speeches 1979–1995.* Princeton, NJ: Carnegie Foundation for the Advancement of Teaching, 1997.

Brookfield, S. "Using Critical Incidents to Explore Learners' Assumptions." In Mezirow and Associates, *Fostering Critical Reflection in Adulthood: A Guide to Transformative and Emancipatory Learning* (pp. 177–193). San Francisco: Jossey-Bass, 1990.

Brookfield, S. D. *Becoming a Critically Reflective Teacher.* San Francisco: Jossey-Bass, 1995.

Brookfield, S. D. *Skillful Teacher: On Techniques, Trust, and Responsiveness in the Classroom.* 2nd ed. San Francisco: Jossey-Bass, 2006.

Brown, R. *If at First You Do Not See.* New York: Henry Holt, 1982.

Bruner, J. *Acts of Meaning.* Cambridge: Harvard University Press, 1990.

Bruner, J. "Life as Narrative." In Dyson, A. H., and Genishi, C. (eds.), *The Need for Story: Cultural Diversity in Classroom and Community* (pp. 28–37). Urbana, IL: National Council of Teachers of English, 1994.

Bruner, J. S. *Making Stories: Law, Literature, Life.* New York: Farrar, Strauss, Giroux, 2002.

Campbell, W. G. *Form and Style in Thesis Writing.* 2nd ed. Boston: Houghton Mifflin, 1954.

Carrell, L. A. "Scholarly Teaching Adventure. . ." *International Journal for the Scholarship of Teaching and Learning, 1*(2), July 2007, 1–11. http://www.academics.georgiasouthern.edu/ijsotl/currentv1n2.htm [Accessed November 6, 2012]

Cisneros, S. *The House on Mango Street.* New York: Alfred A. Knopf, 1984.

Connelly, F. M., and Clandinin, D. J. "Stories of Experience and Narrative Inquiry." *Educational Researcher,* June-July 1990, *19*(5), 2–14.

Connelly, F. M., and Clandinin, D. J. "Composing, Sustaining, and Changing Stories." In Connelly, F. M., and Clandinin, D. J. (eds.), *Shaping a Professional Identity: Stories of Educational Practice* (pp. 94–102). New York: Teachers College Press, 1999.

Corrigan, P. T. "How I Came to Understand That My Students Would Need Training Wings in Order to Learn to Fly." *College Teaching,* 2011, *59,* 127–128.

Corsini, R. J., and Howard, D. D. (eds.). *Critical Incidents in Teaching.* Englewood Cliffs, NJ: Prentice Hall, 1964.

Cortazzi, M. *Narrative Analysis.* London: Falmer Press, 1993.

Cox, J. R. "Lessons from Room 10." *Teaching Professor,* May 2011, *25*(5), 6.

Crites, S. "The Narrative Quality of Experience." *Journal of American Academy of Religion.* September 1971, *39,* 291–311.

Denzin, N. K. *Interpretive Biography.* Qualitative Research Series 17. Newbury Park, CA: Sage, 1989.

Dewey, J. *How We Think.* Boston: D. C. Heath, 1910.

Dickens, C. *Hard Times.* Enriched Classics Edition. New York: Pocket Books, 2007 (Originally published 1854).

Doll, M. A. *Like Letters in Running Water: A Mythopoetics of Curriculum.* Mahwah, NJ: Lawrence Erlbaum, 2000.

Duarte, F. "Using Autoethnography in the Scholarship of Teaching and Learning: Reflective Practice from 'the Other Side of the Mirror.'" *International Journal for the Scholarship of Teaching and Learning*, July 2007, *1*(2), 1–11. http://www.academics.georgiasouthern.edu/ijsotl/currentv1n2 .htm [Accessed November 6, 2012]

Eakin, P. J. *Living Autobiographically: How We Create Identity in Narrative*. Ithaca, NY: Cornell University Press, 2008.

Edwards, N. M. "Student Self-Grading in Social Statistics." *College Teaching*, 2007, *55*(2), 72–76.

Ferguson, W. 'I Don't Know What I Mean Until I See What I Say': The Need to Incorporate the Effects of Language Generation on the Speaker. No date. http://csc.media.mit.edu/iuiStories/papers/Ferguson.pdf. [Retrieved June 30, 2011.]

Flanagan, J. C. "The Critical Incident Technique." *Psychological Bulletin*, 1954, *51*(4), 327–358.

Freeman, P. R., and Schmidt, J. Z. (eds.). *Wise Women: Reflections of Teachers at Midlife*. New York: Routledge, 2002.

Freire, P. *Pedagogy of Freedom: Ethics, Democracy, and Civic Courage*. Lanham, MD: Rowman & Littlefield, 1998.

Freire, P. *Pedagogy of the Oppressed*. Tr. M. B. Tamos. 20th Anniversary Edition. New York, New York: Continuum, 1993.

Glück, L. "Education of the Poet." In *Proofs and Theories: Essays on Poetry* (pp. 3–18). New York: Ecco Press, 1994.

Greene, M. *Teacher as Stranger*. Belmont, CA: Wadsworth, 1973.

Greene, M. *Landscapes of Learning*. New York: Teachers College Press, 1978.

Grumet, M. "Existential and Phenomenological Foundations." In Pinar, W., and Grumet, M., *Toward a Poor Curriculum* (pp. 31–50). Dubuque, IA: Kendall/Hunt, 1976.

Grumet, M. "Restitution and Reconstruction of Educational Experience: An Autobiographical Method for Curriculum Theory." In Lawn, M., and Barton, L. (eds.), *Rethinking Curriculum Studies: A Radical Approach* (pp. 115–130). New York: John Wiley and Sons, 1981.

Gudmundsdottir, S. "Story-Maker, Story-Teller: Narrative Structures in Curriculum." *Journal of Curriculum Studies*, 1991, *23*, 207–218.

Gunn, J. V. *Autobiography: Toward a Poetics of Experience*. Philadelphia: University of Pennsylvania Press, 1982.

Hall, S. S. "J. Mercator." In K. Harmon, *You Are Here: Personal Geographies and Other Maps of the Imagination*. New York: Princeton Architectural Press, 2004.

Hawk, T. F., and Lyons, P. R. "Please Don't Give Up on Me: When Faculty Fail to Care." *Journal of Management Education*, 2008, *32*(3), 316–338.

Heaney, S. "Seamus Heaney—Nobel Lecture." Nobelprize.org, 1995 http://www .nobelprize.org/nobel_prizes/literature/laureates/1995/heaney-lecture .html.

Herreid, C. F. (ed.). *Start with a Story: The Case Study Method of Teaching College Science*. Arlington, VA: National Science Teachers Association, 2007.

Hickson, H. "Critical Reflection: Reflecting on Learning to Be Reflective." *Reflective Practice*, December 2011, *12*(6), 829–839.

hooks, b. *Teaching Critical Thinking: Practical Wisdom*. New York: Routledge, 2010.

Ibsen, H. *Peet Gynt*. C. Fry and J. Fillinger, Trans. World's Classic Edition. Oxford, England: Oxford University Press, 1992 [1867].

Jalongo, M. R., and Isenberg, J. P. *Teachers' Stories: From Personal Narrative to Professional Insight*. San Francisco: Jossey-Bass, 1995.

Jones, T. B. "My Best College Teachers." *National Teaching & Learning Forum*. March 2010, *19*(3), 6–7.

Jordan, H. *Mudbound*. Chapel Hill, NC: Algonquin, 2008.

Khazanov, L. "When an Instructor Must Take the Back Seat." *PRIMUS*, 2007, *XVII*(2), 157–166.

Kher, N., Molstad, S., and Donahue, R. "Using Humor in the College Classroom to Enhance Teaching Effectiveness in 'Dread Courses.'" *College Student Journal*, 1999, *33*(3), 400–406.

Killen, R., and McKee, A. *Critical Incidents in Teaching: An Approach to Teacher Decision-Making*. Newcastle, Australia: Newcastle Collection of Advanced Education, 1983.

Killick, S., and Frude, N. "The Teller, the Tale, and the Told." *The Psychologist*, October 2009, *22*(Part 10), 850–853.

Kuhn, T. S. *The Structure of Scientific Revolutions*. Chicago: University of Chicago Press, 1970 [1962].

Lawrence-Lightfoot, S. L. *The Essential Conversation: What Parents and Teachers Can Learn from Each Other*. New York: Random House, 2003.

Lessing, D. *Prisons We Choose to Live Inside*. Hammersmith, London: Flamingo, 1994.

Lewis, S. E., and Lewis, J. E. "Departing From Lectures: An Evaluation of Peer-Led Guided Inquiry Alternative." *Journal of Chemical Education*, 2005, *82*(1), 135–139.

Lobel, A. "The Lobster and the Crab." In *Fables* (p. 8). New York: Harper and Row, 1980.

Losee, R. *Doc: Then and Now with a Montana Physician.* New York: Lyons and Burford, 1994.

Loy, D. R. *The World is Made of Stories.* Boston: Wisdom Publications, 2010.

MacDonald, M. P. "It's All in the Past." In Hampel, P., and May, E. T. (eds.), *Tell Me True: A Memoir, History, and Writing a Life* (location 958–1148). St. Paul, MN: Borealis Books, Kindle Edition, 2008.

Maclean, N. *A River Runs Through It and Other Stories.* Chicago: University of Chicago Press, 1976.

Martínez, D. *Breathing Between the Lines.* Tucson: University of Arizona Press, 1997.

Measor, L. "Critical Incidents in the Classroom: Choices and Careers." In Ball, S. J., and Goodson, I. F. (eds.), *Teachers' Lives and Careers* (pp. 61–77). London: Falmer Press, 1985.

Mezirow, J. "How Critical Reflection Triggers Transformative Learning." In Mezirow, J. (ed.), *Fostering Critical Reflection in Adulthood: A Guide to Transformative and Emancipatory Learning* (pp. 1–20). San Francisco: Jossey-Bass, 1990.

Millis, B. J. "Becoming an Effective Teacher Using Cooperative Learning: A Personal Odyssey." *Peer Review*, Spring 2009, *11*(2), 17–21.

Moon, J. A. *Learning Journals: A Handbook for Reflective Practice and Professional Development.* 2nd Ed. London: Routledge, 2006.

Morrison, T. *Nobel Lecture 1993.* New York: Alfred A. Knopf, 1994.

Morrison, T. "The Site of Memory." In Zinsser, W. (ed.), *Inventing the Truth: The Art and Craft of Memoir.* Expanded Edition (pp. 183–200). New York: Houghton Mifflin, 1998.

Nathan, R. *My Freshman Year: What a College Professor Learned by Being a Student.* New York: Penguin, 2005.

Ngan-Ling Chow, E. "Exploring Critical Feminist Pedagogy: Revelation and Confessions about Teaching at Midlife." In Freeman, P. R., and Schmidt, J. Z. (eds.), *Wise Women: Reflections of Teachers at Midlife* (pp. 197–210). New York: Routledge, 2002.

Palmer, P. *Courage to Teach.* 10th Anniversary Edition. San Francisco: Jossey-Bass, 2007.

Pinar, W. "Autobiography and the Architecture of Self." *Journal of Curriculum Theorizing*, 1988, 8(1), 7–35.

Polkinghorne, D. E. *Narrative Knowing and the Human Sciences.* Albany: State University of New York Press, 1988.

Pratt, D. "Analyzing Perspectives: Identifying Commitments and Belief Structures." In Pratt, D., & Associates, *Five Perspectives on Teaching in*

Adult and Higher Education (pp. 217–255). Malabar, FL: Krieger, 1998.

Reason, P., and Hawkins, P. "Storytelling as Inquiry." In Reason, P. (ed.), *Human Inquiry in Action: Developments in New Paradigm Research* (pp. 79–101). London: Sage, 1988.

Rheingold, H. *They Have a Word for It: A Lighthearted Lexicon of Untranslatable Words & Phrases*. Louisville, KY: Sarabande Books, 1988.

Rich, A. "Twenty-One Love Poems XIII." In *The Dream of a Common Language: Poems 1974–1977* (p. 31). New York: W.W. Norton, 1978.

Rich, A. "An Atlas of the Difficult World." In *An Atlas of the Difficult World: Poems 1988–1991* (pp. 3–26). New York: W.W. Norton, 1991.

Rolfe, G., Jasper, M., and Freshwater, D. *Critical Reflection in Practice: Generating Knowledge for Care*. 2nd ed. New York: Palgrave Macmillan, 2011.

Rosenshine, B., and Meister, C. "The Use of Scaffolds for Teaching Higher-Level Cognitive Strategies." *Educational Leadership*, 1992, 49(7), 26–33.

Rowe, M. B. "Wait-Time and Rewards as Instructional Variables: Their Influence on Language, Logic, and Fate Control." April 1972. Paper presented at the National Association for Research in Science Teaching, Chicago. ED 061103.

Sanders, S. R. *Staying Put: Making a Home in a Restless World*. Boston: Beacon Press, 1993.

Sanders, S. R. "The Power of Stories." In *The Force of Spirit* (pp. 82–101). Boston: Beacon, 2000.

Sandstrom, K. L. "Embracing Modest Hopes: Lessons from the Beginning of a Teaching Journey." In Pescosolido, B. A., and Aminzade, R. (eds.), *The Social Worlds of Higher Education: Handbook for Teaching in a New Century* (pp. 517–529). Thousand Oaks, CA: Pine Forge Press, 1999.

Sattlemeyer, R. (General Editor), and O'Connell, P. F. (Editor). *The Writing of Henry D. Thoreau: Journal*, vol. 5: 1852–1853. Princeton, NJ: Princeton University Press, 1997.

Schlink, B. *The Reader*. Tr. Carol Brown Janeway. New York: Vintage, 1998.

Schwab, J. "The Practical 3: Translation into the Curriculum." *School Review*, August 1973, 81(4), 501–522.

Schön, D. A. *The Reflective Practitioner: How Professionals Think in Action*. New York: Basic Books, 1983.

Schön, D. A. *Educating the Reflective Practitioner*. San Francisco: Jossey-Bass, 1987.

Schön, D. A., and Rein, M. *Frame Reflection: Toward the Resolution of Intractable Policy Controversies.* New York: Basic Books, 1994.

Searby, L. J., and Tripses, J. S. "Going to the Balcony: Two Professors Reflect and Examine Their Pedagogy." *International Journal for the Scholarship of Teaching and Learning,* January 2011, 5(1). http://academics .georgiasouthern.edu/ijsotl/v5n1/essays_about_sotl/PDFs/_SearbyTripses .pdf. [Accessed January 17, 2012.]

Shadiow, L. "My Students as My Teachers." *Clearing House,* 1985, 58(83), 232–233.

Shadiow, L. "Remembrances: Miss Hentges." *College Board Review,* Fall 1985, 137, 32–33.

Shadiow, L. "The Legacy of Teacher Comments." *English Journal,* January 2007, 96(3), 15–16.

Shadiow, L. "First Day of Class: How It Matters." *Clearing House,* 2009, 84(4), 197–199.

Shadiow, L. "In Praise of Cacophony." *National Teaching & Learning Forum,* December 2009, 19(1), 4–6.

Shadiow, L. "Disrupting Charted Systems: Identifying and Deconstructing Critical Incidents in Teaching." *Journal on Excellence in College Teaching,* 2010, 21(3), 63–72.

Shadiow, L. "Classroom Interactions: Constructing a Room with a View." *College Teaching,* April-June 2010, 58(2), 58–61.

Shields, C. *Larry's Party.* New York: Penguin, 1998.

Sikes, A. L., Measor, L., and Woods, P. *Teachers' Careers: Crisis and Continuities.* London: Falmer Press, 1985.

Smith, A. M. *The Charming Quirks of Others.* New York: Pantheon, Kindle Edition, 2010.

Smith, M. K. "Chris Argyris: Theories of Action, Double-loop Learning and Organizational Learning." *Encyclopedia of Informal Learning,* 2001. [http://www.infed.org/thinkers/argyris.htm].

Spence, L. D. "Drill and Practice." *Teaching Professor.* October 2009, 23 (8), 5.

Starcher, K. "Imposter with the Roster: How I Gave Up Control and Became a Better Teacher." *Teaching Professor,* October 2010, 24(8), 1, 5.

Stegner, W. E. *Angle of Repose.* New York: Penguin, 1971.

Stenberg, S. J. *Professing and Pedagogy: Learning the Teaching of English.* Urbana, IL: National Council of Teachers of English, 2005.

Tagg, J. *The Learning Paradigm College.* Bolton, MA: Anker Publishing, 2003.

Tanner, K. D. "Moving Theory into Practice: A Reflection on Teaching a Large, Introductory Biology Course for Majors." *CBE – Life Sciences Education*, Summer 2011, *101*, 113–122.

Taylor, C. *Multiculturalism and the Politics of Recognition: An Essay*. Princeton, NJ: Princeton University Press, 1992.

Tompkins, J. P. *A Life in School: What the Teacher Learned*. New York: Perseus Books, 1996.

Torres, C. A. *Education, Power, and Personal Biography*. New York: Routledge, 1998.

Tripp, D. *Critical Incidents in Teaching: Developing Professional Judgment*. London: Routledge, 1993.

van Manen, M. "Pedagogy, Virtue, and Narrative Identity in Teaching." *Curriculum Inquiry*, 1994, *24*(2), 135–170.

Watson, C. "'Teachers Are Meant To Be Orthodox': Narrative and Counter Narrative in the Discursive Construction of 'Identity' in Teaching." *International Journal of Qualitative Studies in Education*. July-August 2009, *22*(4), 469–483.

Webster, L., and Mertova, P. *Using Narrative Inquiry as a Research Method: An Introduction to Using Critical Event Narrative Analysis in Research on Learning and Teaching*. London: Routledge, 2007.

Weeber, S. C. "'Critically Reflective Pedagogy': Teaching Sociology After Hurricanes Katrina and Rita." *Journal of Sociology, Social Work and Social Welfare*, 2011, *2*(1), 1–18 http://www.scientificjournals.org/Journals 2011/articles/1489.pdf. [Accessed March 2, 2012.]

Weimer, M. *Learner-Centered Teaching: Five Key Changes to Practice*. San Francisco: Jossey-Bass, 2002.

Weimer, M. *Inspired College Teaching: A Career-long Resource for Professional Growth*. San Francisco: Jossey-Bass, 2010.

Welch, S. D. *Sweet Dreams in America: Making Ethics and Spirituality Work*. New York: Routledge, 1999.

Wilson, S. *Research Is Ceremony: Indigenous Research Methods*. Halifax, Nova Scotia: Fernwood, 2008.

Wood, D. R. "Narrating Professional Development: Teachers' Stories as Texts for Improving Practice." *Anthropology & Education Quarterly*, December 2000, *31*(4), 426–448.

Woods, P. *Critical Events in Teaching and Learning*. London: Falmer Press, 1993.

Yanchar, S. C., and Slife, B. D. "Teaching Critical Thinking by Examining Assumptions." *Teaching of Psychology*, 2004, *31*(2), 85–90.

Index

A

Acts of Meaning (Bruner), 65
Adams, D., 80, 116
"Alexander Solzhenitsyn's Literature and
   Politics" (hypothetical course), 12–13
Allende, I., 59, 63
Allison, D., 169
Angle of Repose (Stegner), 21, 23
"The architecture of self," 36
Argyris, C., 22
Assumptions: analyzing incidents for,
   116–122; using critical incidents to
   identify, 107–111; critical reflection
   required for understanding influence
   of, 126–127; defining, 111–112;
   influence of contexts on, 116,
   133–134; interactions among different
   categories of, 128–134; made through
   process of locating claims, 91, 101;
   process of identifying, 119–122; three
   categories of, 101, 112–116. *See also*
   Casual assumptions; Paradigmatic
   assumptions; Prescriptive assumptions
Autobiographical stories. *See* Educational
   biographies; Living stories

B

Bain, K., 22, 103, 122, 126
Ball, S. J., 48
"Banking concept" of students, 37–38
Banks, R., 84
Barr, R., 18, 19, 20
"Because" statements, 59–60, 69, 129,
   152

Becoming a Critically Reflective Teacher
   (Brookfield), 22, 101, 112
"Becoming an Effective Teacher Using
   Cooperative Learning: A Personal
   Odyssey" (Millis), 168
Beliefs. *See* Paradigmatic assumptions
Berry, W., 63
Boyer, E., 32–33
Breathing Between the Lines (Martínez),
   11, 78–79
"Bringing Questions to Freire" story:
   events of, 38–40; expectations and
   peripeteia in the, 60; learner role in
   the, 74; role of content within, 76; role
   of teacher in, 72; as story from
   professional venue, 42; symbol coding
   used in, 53
Brookfield, S. D., 5, 22, 48, 96, 100, 101,
   112, 114, 143, 158, 161–162
Brown, R., 129, 141
Bruner, J., 60, 65, 87, 103, 107, 116, 146,
   157

C

Campbell, W. G., 155
Carnegie Foundation for the
   Advancement of Teaching, 32,
   33
Carrell, L., 49
Causal assumptions: description of, 101,
   113, 130–131; examining Corrigan's,
   117, 118; exercise on exploring critical
   incidents for prescriptive and,
   134–137; "First Day" story, 138;

Causal assumptions (*Continued*)
interrelationship between prescriptive
and, 132–134; of "Mr. Berg's
Comment" story, 157, 167; on peer-led
work leading to student-to-student
interaction, 132; process of identifying,
120–121. *See also* Assumptions;
Expectations
Chow, E.N.-L., 50
Cisneros, S., 145
Claims: articulated through critical
incidents, 87–91; assumptions made
through locating, 91, 101; embedded
within your critical incidents, 96–98;
examples of locating and making,
91–96; naming the, 98–100; the
personal mapmaking we undertake to
make, 94; P.S. 98 story on teacher's,
92–93
Clandinin, D. J., 56
"Classroom Interactions: Constructing a
Room with a View" (Shadiow), 160
Classrooms: building "democratic
reconstruction" of environment for,
162; how narratives transverse our, 26;
how students bring their individual
stories into the, 15–16; Millis' essay
chronicling her evolving journey in
the, 168; story-making and
story-telling dimensions of, 26–27;
wait-time during discussions in, 35–36
Cloudsplitter (Banks), 84
Codes. *See* Symbolic codes
College English journal, 132
College Teaching journal, 116, 133
College Training journal, 132
Commonplaces: description of, 70; role of
content in critical incidents, 75–76;
role of learner in critical incidents,
73–75; role of teacher in critical
incidents, 71–73
Connelly, F. M., 56
Content: claims on meaning of
teaching-learning encounter, 99;
critical incident role of, 75–76; as
element or commonplace of critical
incident, 70; using metaphors to bring
to life, 26
Contexts: filling in the incomplete
information on the, 153–154; influence
on interpretation of teacher role, 146;

influence on the assumptions by, 116,
133–134; influencing the "what" and
"so what" questions of analysis,
146–147; "Mr. Berg's Comment" story
example of layered influences of,
154–158, 163; seeing the contextual
interplay in teaching and learning,
160–164; the self as dependent on,
116
Corrigan, P., 116–117
Corsini, R. J., 47
Cortazzi, M., 46, 123
Cox, J. R., 72
Crites, S., 156
Critical event, 47
Critical incident symbols: applying to
stories, 52–54; coding for and examples
of using, 53–54; descriptive, 51–52;
differentiating between critical
incidents using the, 54–56
Critical incident technique, 47
Critical incident vantage points:
considering the different, 66–68;
determining the initial, 68–70
Critical incidents: analyzed for
assumptions, 116–122; "because"
statements used to describe, 59–60, 69,
129, 152; burrowing process used to
understand, 56; characteristics of a
story on, 47; claims that are articulated
through, 87–91; claims that are
embedded within your, 96–98; defining
terms related to Khazanov's, 46–48;
description of, 106, 142;
differentiating, 54–56; elaborating,
56–61; "excavating" in order to explore
their significance, 74–75; exercise on
exploring causal and prescriptive
assumptions in, 134–137; exploring the
patterns in your, 85–100; identifying
assumptions through, 107–111;
identifying patterns in your, 65–83;
identifying your, 168–169; Khazanov's
description of his own, 45–46, 49, 50;
peripeteia (unexpected reversal of
circumstances) characteristic of, 40,
60; reflection-on-action on, 23, 106;
self-described responses by professors
to, 48–50; telling stories about, 50–51;
three differences in literature context
of, 48; as turning points toward

narrative consciousness, 107–111; vantage points and commonplaces of, 66–78. *See also* Critical reflection; Indelible impressions; Stories; Symbolic codes

Critical incidents commonplaces: role of teacher, 71–73; role of the content, 75–76; role of the learner, 73–75

Critical Incidents in Teaching (Corsini and Howard), 47

Critical Incidents in Teaching (Killen and McKee), 47

Critical Incidents in Teaching (Tripp), 47

Critical Incidents in Teaching (Woods), 47

Critical incidents patterns: considering role patterns across stories, 78–79; considering the vantage points, 66–68; cross-checking stories for, 81–83; determining initial vantage points, 68–70; identifying role of teacher in three critical incidents stories, 79–83; methods used to identify, 69–70; a note on the process of finding, 77–78; the three "commonplaces," 70–76

Critical reflection: cultivated as path toward teaching growth, 8–9; description of, 23; elaboration of codes to understand expectations and peripeteia, 60–61; emotional impact of, 50–51, 52; enabling authentic alignment of action and intention, 123; heuristic process of, 61–62, 63; how teaching is enlightened through process of, 4–5; how truths about teaching practices is revealed by, 140–141; "indelible impressions" of, 45, 51–52; Khazanov on incident that triggered his, 45–46; mining metaphor of, 111–112; "pay attention" element of, 63; prompts for structured guidance for recalling and, 62; symbolic codes used for, 52–61; understanding that there a multiple ways for, 61; understanding the influence of assumptions through, 126–127. *See also* Critical incidents

"Critical Reflection: Reflecting on Learning to be Reflective" (Hickson), 162

"'Critically Reflective Pedagogy': Teaching Sociology after Hurricanes Katrina and Rita" (Weeber), 161

Curriculum vita as story, 10–12

D

Daily story-making: curriculum vita used as story in, 10–12; examining your own practice of, 9; intersection between teachers' and students,' 16; "Students Asked Me to Leave" as convergence of, 15; syllabus as story, 12–16

Deliberate practice, 94

Denzin, N. K., 65, 71, 84, 116

Dewey, J., 164–165, 166, 169

Dickens, C., 19

"Doc Story," 66–67

Donahue, R., 119

Double-looped learning, 22, 23

"Drill and Practice" (Spence), 93–94

Duarte, F., 49

E

Eakin, P. J., 47, 142, 145

Educating the Reflective Practitioner (Schön), 17

Educational banking concept, 37–38

Educational biographies: exploring the patterns of, 85–100; identifying patterns in your, 65–83; the table of content for your, 42–43; understanding and decoding your critical incidents, 45–62. *See also* Living stories; Stories; Teaching-learning encounters

Educational biographies commonplaces: description of, 70–71; role of teacher within each critical incident, 71–73; role of the content within each critical incident, 75–76; role of the learner in each critical incident, 73–75

Educational biographies table of content: making sense of your, 42–43; stories from professional venues, 42; stories where I have been a learner, 41–42; stories where I have been a teacher, 42

Edwards, N. M., 133

Elaboration of codes: "because" statements for explaining the story, 59–60, 69, 129, 152; description of process, 58; identifying the major expectation by using the, 60–61;

Elaboration of codes (*Continued*)
"Students Applaud Students" story,
58–59
"Embracing Modest Hopes: Lessons from
the Beginning of a Teaching Journey"
(Sandstrom), 160–161
Eva Luna (Allende), 59
Expectations: elaboration used to identify
the major, 60–61; "Mr. Berg's
Comment" story revelation of my, 157;
peripeteia (unexpected reversal of
circumstances) used with, 60; Tanner
on her critical reflections on, 144. *See
also* Causal assumptions
Exploratory mission process: description
of, 28; on memories of our professional
life, 37–41; on our lives as teachers,
33–37; for remembering experience of
being a student, 31–33

F

Fables (Lobel children's book), 91
Ferguson, W., 51
"First Day" story: because statements used
to understand, 152; casual,
prescriptive, and paradigmatic
assumptions in, 137–138; events of,
108–109; how contexts influenced
interpretation of teacher role, 146;
identified as critical incident, 107–111,
168; as story where I have been a
teacher, 42; symbolic codes found in
the, 55; three assumptions in the,
114–116; two contrasting paradigmatic
assumptions in, 128
Fitzgerald, Z., 35
Flanagan, J. C., 47
Form and Style in Theses (Campbell), 155
*Frame Reflection: Toward the Resolution of
Intractable Policy Controversies* (Schön
and Rein), 17, 18
Frame reflection concept, 17–18, 21, 23
Free play, 269–270
Freeman, P. R., 50
Freire, P., 37, 67, 147, 153, 168
Freshwater, D., 107, 145
Frude, N., 51

G

"Geologic Disasters" course, 26, 27
Glück, L., 45, 51, 62

"Going to the Balcony: Two Professors
Reflect and Examine Their Pedagogy"
(Searby and Tripses), 136, 137, 166
"Going to the balcony" process, 136, 137,
166
Goodson, F., 48
"Grad School Decision" story: basic
themes shared by "Winter Saturday
Classroom" and, 8; events of, 7–8;
as story where I have been a learner,
42
Greene, M., 5, 31, 43, 44
Grumet, M., 46, 71, 74–75, 79, 85, 102,
111
Gudmundsdottir, S., 26, 43
Gunn, J. V., 121

H

Hall, S. S., 94, 96
Hard Times (Dickens), 19
Hawk, T., 49, 50
Hawkins, P., 47
Heaney, S., 127
Herreid, C. F., 119
Heuristic reflection process, 61–62, 63
Hickson, H., 122, 162–163, 165
The Hitchhiker's Guide to the Galaxy
(Adams), 80, 116
hooks, b., 25, 96
The House on Mango Street (Cisneros),
145
"How I Came to Understand That My
Students Would Need Training Wings
in Order to Learn to Fly" (Corrigan),
116–117
How We Think (Dewey), 164–165
Howard, D. D., 47

I

Ibsen, H., 43
If At First You Do Not See (Brown), 129,
141
Indelible impressions: articulating the
specific responses that create, 51–52;
created through images in stories,
87–88; Khazanov's story on an incident
leaving an, 45–46; new awareness
developed through, 62–63; P.S. 98
story on teacher claims making an,
92–93. *See also* Critical incidents
Inspired College Teaching (Weimer), 141

Instruction-centered pedagogy:
comparing learner-centered to, 18, 20;
literature on, 18–19; shifting to
learner-centered from, 20–21
Intentions: learning to move past your,
167; tension between teaching action
and, 122, 137, 164–165, 167
Iron Range (Northern Minnesota),
111
Isenberg, J. P., 49, 52, 61, 71

J

Jalongo, M. R., 49, 52, 61, 71
Jasper, M., 107, 145
Jones, T. B., 94–95
Jordan, H., 123
Journal of Chemical Education, 132
Journal of Engineering Education,
132
Journal of Geoscience Education, 132

K

Kaleidoscope metaphor, 149, 150,
152–153, 169
Khazanov, L., 45–46, 49, 50
Kher, N., 119
Killen, R., 47
Killick, R., 51
"Kirby's Paper" story: as educational
biography story, 8; growing meaning
and significance of retelling, 33, 50–51;
on interaction between teacher and
student, 16; as story where I have been
a teacher, 42
Knowledge-in-action, 23, 123
Kuhn, T., 128

L

Lawrence-Lightfoot, S., 6, 28
Learner-centered pedagogy: comparing
instruction-centered to, 18–19;
literature on, 18, 20; shifting from
instruction-centered to, 20–21
*Learner-Centered Teaching: Five Key
Changes to Practice* (Weimer), 20
Learner stories: "Grad School Decision,"
7–8, 42; memories of our experience as
basis for, 31–33, 41–42; "Miss
Hentges's Recognition," 29–31, 41;
"Mr. Berg's Comment," 42, 154–158,
160, 163, 167

Learners: college as institution aiming to
produce, 20; critical incident role of,
73–75. *See also* Students
Learning: as "banking" enterprise, 38;
college as institution aiming to
produce, 20; contextual interplay in
teaching and, 160–164; double-looped,
22, 23; how deliberate practice can
ruin, 94; paradigmatic assumption that
supportive recognition is key to, 158;
prescriptive assumption on
student-to-student interactions and,
132–133; single-loop, 22, 23. *See also*
Teaching-learning encounters
"Learning About Oneself as a Teacher"
(Sandstrom), 161
The Learning Paradigm College (Tagg),
18
Lessing, D., 80–81
"Lessons from Room 10" (Cox), 72, 74,
76
Lewis, J. E., 132
Lewis, S. E., 132
"Library Firing" story: events of, 10–11; as
story from professional venue, 42
A Life in School: What a Teacher Learned
(Tompkins), 28, 50, 92
*Living Autobiographically: How We Create
Identity in Narrative* (Eakin), 145
Living stories: foundations of, 27–31;
memories of being a student basis of,
31–33; of our lives as teachers, 33–37;
from the professional arena we work in,
37–41; repertoire or table of contents
of your, 41–43. *See also* Educational
biographies
Living stories foundations: being a
student experience used as, 31–33;
being a teacher experience used as,
33–37; "Bringing Questions to Freire"
story example of using, 38–40, 55,
57–59, 60, 72, 74, 76; examining the
experiences that create, 27–31; "Miss
Hentges's Recognition" story example
of using, 29–31, 41; professional arena
experience used for, 37–41; "Using
Wait-time" story example of using,
35–36, 42
Living stories repertoire: stories from
professional venues, 42; stories where I
have been a learner, 41–42;

Living stories repertoire (*Continued*)
stories where I have been a teacher, 42; where I have been a learner, 41–42
Loy, D. R., 97, 104
Lyons, P. R., 49

M

MacDonald, M. P., 34
MacLean, N., 3, 4, 122
Martínez, D., 11, 78–79
McKee, A., 47
Measor, L., 47, 142
Meister, C., 61
Merchant of Venice (Shakespeare), 94
Mertova, P., 47, 48, 55, 98
Metaphors: bringing content to life through, 26; kaleidoscope, 149, 150, 152–153, 169; mining, 111–112; orienteering, 94, 96; purposeful reflection, 41; "Students Applaud Students" story on creating the best, 57–58; weaving, 85–86
Mezirow, J., 167
Millis, B., 168
Mining metaphor of critical reflection, 111–112
"Miss Hentges's Recognition" story: events of, 29–31; as story where I have been a learner, 41
Molstad, S., 119
Moon, J. A., 100
Morrison, T., 15, 40, 100
"Moving Theory into Practice: A Reflection on Teaching a Large Introductory Biology Course for Majors" (Tanner), 144
"Mr. Berg's Comment" story: assumptions of, 157, 167; events of, 42; layered influences of contexts in, 154–158, 163; linking teaching to intention as originating from, 160; as story where I have been a learner, 42
Mudbound (Jordan), 123
Multiculturalism and the Politics of Recognition (Taylor), 167
"My Best College Teachers" (Jones), 94–95
My Freshman Year: What a College Professor Learned by Being a Student (Nathan), 16

N

Narratives: critical incidents as turning points toward, 107–111; history of identities in, 101; how they transverse our classrooms, 26. See also Stories
Nathan, R., 16
Natural Critical Learning Environment, 103–104, 122–123, 126

O

Orienteering metaphor, 94, 96

P

Palmer, P., 5
Paradigm, 128
Paradigmatic assumptions: deeper view of origins and choices through, 123, 127–128; definition of, 128–129; description of, 101, 114; examining Corrigan's, 117, 118; "First Day" story as example of two contrasting, 128, 138; influence on our teaching practices by, 126, 128; insights possible through examining, 118–119; of "Mr. Berg's Comment" story, 157, 167; persistence of, 143–145; process of identifying, 138–143; on supportive recognition as key to learning, 158. See also Assumptions
Paying attention, 63
Pedagogies: "going to the balcony" process of examining one's, 136, 137, 166; instruction-centered, 18–19, 20–21; learner-centered, 18, 20–21; of supportive recognition as being key to learning, 158; value of ongoing dialogue between learned and enacted, 86–87. See also Teaching practices
Pedagogy of the Oppressed (Freire), 37
"Pedagogy, Virtue, and Narrative Identity in Teaching" (van Manen), 24
Peer Gynt (Ibsen), 43
"Perception of Credibility" story: "going to the balcony" using the, 166–167; intersection of intentions and actions related to teaching in, 158–160; as story from professional venue, 42; symbolic codes found in the, 55
Peripeteia (unexpected reversal of circumstances), 40, 60
Pinar, W., 36, 77

Plath, S., 35
Playing, 269–270
Politics of recognition: in classrooms where you were a student, 31–33; description of, 30; in our lives as teachers, 33–37; within the professional arena, 37–41
Polkinghorne, D. E., 63
Power dynamics: of classroom student and teacher roles, 31–37; of politics of recognition, 30; professional, 37–41; tension theme of power and, 165–166
Pratt, D., 111, 114
Prescriptive assumptions: description of, 101, 113–114, 131; examining Corrigan's, 117, 118; exercise on exploring critical incidents for causal and, 134–137; "First Day" story, 138; interrelationship between causal and, 132–134; of "Mr. Berg's Comment" story, 157, 167; process of identifying, 121–122. *See also* Assumptions; Values
Prisons We Choose to Live Inside (Lessing), 80–81
Professing and Pedagogy (Stenberg), 86
Professional venues stories: "Bringing Questions to Freire," 38–40, 42, 55, 60, 72, 74, 76; curriculum vita as, 10–12; examples of, 42; forming a "hidden curriculum" in our professional development, 71; "Library Firing," 10–11, 42; "Perception of Credibility," 42, 55, 158–160; professional writing as, 17; syllabus as, 12–16; "Walk with Sharon," 42
Professional writing as story, 17
P.S. 98, 92–93
Purposeful reflection metaphor, 41

R

Reason, P., 47
Reflection. *See* Critical reflection
Reflection-on-action, 23, 106
The Reflective Practitioner: How Professionals Think in Action (Schön), 17
Reflective thinking: the free play of, 169–170; what is required for, 165
Rein, M., 17, 18
Research Is Ceremony: Indigenous Research Methods (Wilson), 77, 163–164

Retelling story accounts: different forms used for, 50; differentiating critical incidents when, 54–56; elaborating critical incidents during process of, 56–61; emotional responses and reflections when, 48–50; indelible impressions included in the, 45, 51–52, 62; symbolic coding used for analysis when, 51–59; terms related to critical reflection when, 46–48
Rich, A., 68, 125
A River Runs Through It and Other Stories (MacLean), 122
Rolfe, G., 107, 145
Rorschach inkblot, 116
Rosenshine, B., 61
Rowe, M. B., 34, 35

S

Sage on the Stage model, 5, 8
Sanders, S. R., 41, 89, 167
Sandstrom, K., 160–161, 162
Sattlemeyer, R., 126
Schlink, B., 109
Schmidt, J. Z., 50
Schön, D. A., 5, 17, 18, 22, 78, 106, 123, 157
Schwab, J., 70, 73
Searby, L. J., 136, 137, 166
"Self now": description and story presentation of the, 65, 66; "Mr. Berg's Comment" story's perception by, 157; shifting meanings of your, 97–98; vantage point of the, 71
"Self then": description and story presentation of the, 65, 66; "Mr. Berg's Comment" story's perception by, 157; shifting meanings of your, 97–98; vantage point of the, 71
Self/selves: as context-dependent, 116; our teaching self, 36; retelling a story and presentation of the four different, 65–66
Sexton, A., 35
Shadiow, L., 3, 30, 109, 156, 160
Shields, C., 98–99
"Shoulder-Shrugger" story: articulating claims through telling of the, 89–90; as collection of pivotal incidents, 144; used as cross-check for critical incident patterns, 81–83; events of, 81–82;

"Shoulder-Shrugger" story (*Continued*)
similarities between "Students Asked
Me to Leave" and, 90; as story where I
have been a teacher, 42; symbolic
codes found in the, 55
SIETAR conference (1992), 38
Sikes, A. L., 47, 142
Single-loop learning, 22, 23
"The Site of Memory" (Morrison), 100
Slife, B. D., 112
Smith, A. M., 98
Smith, M. K., 22
"Sociology of Everyday Life" course,
161
Solzhenitsyn, A., 12
Spence, L., 93–94, 95, 100
Starcher, K., 5–6
*Start with a Story: The Case Study Method
of Teaching College Science* (Herreid),
119
*Staying Put: Making a Home in a Restless
World* (Sanders), 41, 167
Stegner, W., 21
Stenberg, S., 86–87, 164
Storied foundations: being a student
experience used as, 31–33; being a
teacher experience used as, 33–37;
"Bringing Questions to Freire" story
example of using, 38–40, 42, 55, 60,
72, 74, 76; examining the experiences
that create, 27–31; "Miss Hentges's
Recognition" story example of using,
29–30, 41; professional arena
experience used for, 37–41; "Using
Wait-time" story example of using,
35–36, 42
Stories: as being *about* us and also *are* us,
145; choices and values impacting the
line of action (or plot) of, 98;
considering role patterns across all,
78–79; daily story-making, 9–16;
imperatives for paying attention to, 63;
indelible impressions left by, 45, 51–52,
62; living, 25–44; recalling storied
accounts, 45–63; story-making and
story-telling dimensions of, 26–27, 43;
vantage points and commonplaces in,
66–77; weaving metaphor of, 85–86.
See also Critical incidents; Educational
biographies; Narratives
Story-making dimension, 26–27, 43

Story patterns: determining the initial
vantage points, 68–70; methods for
examining your educational
biographies and finding, 69–70;
vantage points, 66–68
Story-telling dimension, 26–27, 43
Story titles: "Bringing Questions to
Freire," 38–40, 42, 55, 60, 72, 74, 76;
"First Day," 42, 55, 107–111, 114–116,
128, 137–138, 146, 152, 168; "Grad
School Decision," 7–8, 42; "Kirby's
Paper," 8, 16, 33, 42, 50–51; "Lessons
from Room 10" (Cox), 72, 74, 76;
"Library Firing," 10–11, 42; "Miss
Hentges's Recognition," 29–31, 41;
"Mr. Berg's Comment," 42, 154–158,
160, 163, 167; "Perception of
Credibility," 42, 55, 158–160;
"Shoulder-Shrugger," 42, 55, 81–82,
89–90, 144; "Students Applaud
Students," 42, 55, 57–59, 68–69, 72,
74, 75–76, 79, 87, 140, 144, 150–153;
"Students Asked Me to Leave," 13–15,
19, 22, 33, 42, 46, 52, 55, 79, 90, 144,
145–146, 168; "Using Wait-time,"
35–36, 42; "Walk with Sharon" story,
42; "Winter Saturday Classroom," 3–4,
8, 18, 19, 33, 42, 53, 70–71
"Storytelling as Inquiry" (Reason and
Hawkins), 47
The Structure of Scientific Revolutions
(Kuhn), 128
"Student Self-Grading in Social
Statistics" (Edwards), 133
Students: "banking concept" perception
of, 37–38; claims on what it means to
be a, 99; intersection between the
stories of teachers' and their, 1;
memories of our experience as, 31–33,
41–42; "Students Asked Me to Leave"
as convergences of stories by, 15. *See
also* Learners
"Students Applaud Students" story: as
collection of pivotal incidents, 144;
context of, 153; creating the "best"
metaphor in, 57–58; determining the
initial vantage points in, 68–69;
dormant assumption in, 140;
elaboration of the codes for, 58–59;
events of, 57–59; expectations and
peripeteia found in, 60; individual and

cumulative surprises of each stage using the, 150–153; revealing the hidden layers of, 87; role of content within the, 75–76; role of teacher in the, 72; role of the learner in, 74; as story where I have been a teacher, 42; symbolic codes found in the, 55; symbolic coding used to examine critical incident of, 58–59; vantage point and teacher role in, 79

"Students Asked Me to Leave" story: as catalyst for reflection, 22, 46; as collection of pivotal incidents, 144; discovery of a teaching value through the, 145–146; events of, 13–15; growing meaning and significance of, 33; identifying as a critical incident, 168; similar expectations in "Winter Saturday Classroom" and, 19; similarities between "Shoulder-Shrugger" and, 90; as story where I have been a teacher, 42; symbolic codes of critical incident during, 52, 53–54, 55; vantage point and teacher role in, 79

Syllabus as story, 12–16

Symbolic codes: "because" statements added to each, 59–60, 69, 129, 152; to differentiate critical incidents, 54–56; used for each critical incident, 53; elaboration of the, 58–61; how to apply the, 52–54; identifying assumptions through the, 129; as representing a type of response to the story, 52; "Students Applaud Students" elaboration of the, 58–59. See also Critical incidents

T

Tagg, J., 18, 19, 20

Tanner, K. D., 143–144

Taylor, C., 30, 167

Teacher Professor (Starcher), 6

Teacher stories: "First Day," 42, 55, 107–111, 114–116, 128, 137–138, 146, 152, 168; "Kirby's Paper," 8, 16, 33, 42, 50; "Shoulder-Shrugger," 42, 55, 81–82, 89–90, 144; "Students Applaud Students," 42, 55, 57–59, 74, 75–76, 79, 140, 144, 150–153; "Students Asked Me to Leave," 13–15, 19, 22, 33, 42, 46, 52, 55, 72, 79, 90, 144,

145–146, 168; "Using Wait-time," 35–36; "Winter Saturday Classroom," 3–4, 8, 18, 19, 33, 42, 53, 70–71

Teachers: claims on what it means to be a, 99; critical incident role of, 71–73; "First Day" story on context influencing role of, 146; making claims about what it means to be a, 94–95; ongoing dialogue between learned and enacted pedagogies used by, 86–87; paradigmatic assumption on key to learning is supportive recognition by, 158; stories from our life as, 33–37, 42; understanding the foundations of our practices as, 28

Teaching frames: challenge of incorporating pedagogical literature into, 17–18, 21–23; instruction-centered, 18–19; learner-centered, 18, 20; shifting from instruction-centered to learner-centered, 20–21

Teaching-learning encounters: claims on what the content means to, 99; considering role patterns across all stories of, 78–79; considering vantage points and role patterns of the, 66–78; critical incidents, 45–63; examples of role of teacher in three stories of, 79–83; exploring the patterns of your stories of, 85–102; four selves presented during stories of, 65–66; identifying patterns in your stories of, 65–83; *peripeteia* (unexpected reversal of circumstances) in, 40, 60. See also Educational biographies; Learning

Teaching practices: contextual interplay in learning and, 160–164; cultivating reflection as path toward improved, 8–9; goal of becoming conscious of tensions to grow in our, 167–169; how critical reflection reveals truths about, 140–141; influence of paradigmatic assumptions on our, 126, 128; "Perception of Credibility" story on intentions and actions of, 158–160; question and answer wait-time during, 35–36; recognizing the autobiographical roots of our, 6; reflecting on stories to understand our own, 4–5;

Teaching practices (*Continued*)
shifting perspectives experienced
when, 5–9; tension between intention
and action of, 122, 137, 164–166, 167;
tensions related to, 104, 117, 118, 122,
137, 164–167; understanding the
foundations of our practices for, 28.
See also Pedagogies
The Teaching Professor, 72
The teaching self, 36
Teaching Sociology journal, 132
Tensions: control, uncertainty, and
change patterns of, 165; Corrigan on
using reflection and dialogue to
address, 117; goal of grow in our
teaching by becoming conscious of,
167–169; "going to the balcony" to
understand, 136, 137, 166–167;
between intention and action of
teaching, 122, 137, 164–165, 167;
moments of disquieting, 104; power,
control, and expertise themes of,
165–166; recognizing the potential of,
164; reflective thinking for looking
into our, 165; between teaching
practice and underlying belief
structure, 118
Thoreau, H. D., 125–126
Tompkins, J., 28, 31, 50, 92, 95
Torres, C. A., 101
Tripp, D., 47, 50, 51, 107
Tripses, J. S., 136, 137, 166
Two or Three Things I Know for Sure
(Allison), 169

U

U.S. Commissioner of Education, 33
"Using Critical Event Narrative Analysis
in Research on Learning and
Teaching" (Webster and Mertova),
48
"Using Critical Incidents to Explore
Learners' Assumptions" (Brookfield),
48
"Using Humor in the College Classroom
to Enhance Teaching Effectiveness in
'Dread Courses'" (Kher, Molstad, and
Donahue), 119

"Using Wait-time" story: events of,
35–36; as story where I have been a
teacher, 42

V

Values: exploring our assumptions to
expose, 123, 127; "Mr. Berg's
Comment" story revelation of my, 157;
"Students Asked Me to Leave" story on
discovery of, 145–146; Tanner on her
critical reflections on, 144. *See also*
Prescriptive assumptions
van Manen, M., 24
Vantage points: considering the
teaching-learning encounter, 66–68;
determining initial, 68–70; identifying
commonplaces through the, 70–76;
locating a story, 67–68

W

"Walk with Sharon" story, 42
Watson, C., 149, 151
Weaving metaphor of stories, 85–86
Webster, L., 47, 48, 55, 98
Weeber, S., 161, 162
Weimer, M., 9, 20, 23, 115–116, 141
What the Best College Teachers Do (Bain),
22, 103
"When the Instructor Must Take the
Back Seat" (Khazanov), 46
Wilson, S., 69, 77, 163–164
"Winter Saturday Classroom" story: basic
themes shared by "Grad School
Decision" and, 8; beliefs about role as
teacher started with, 18; events of the,
3–4; growing meaning and significance
of, 33; similar expectations in
"Students Asked Me to Leave" and, 19;
as story where I have been a teacher,
42; symbolic codes used to describe
critical incident in, 53, 54; three
commonplaces of the, 70–71
*Wise Women: Reflections of Teachers at
Midlife* (Freeman and Schmidt), 50
Woods, P., 47, 77, 142

Y

Yancher, S. C., 112